Attention and Interest: A Study in Psychology and Education

Felix Arnold

ATTENTION AND INTEREST

THE MACMILLAN COMPANY
NEW YORK · BOSTON · CHICAGO
ATLANTA · SAN FRANCISCO

MACMILLAN & CO., LIMITED
LONDON · BOMBAY · CALCUTTA
MELBOURNE

THE MACMILLAN CO. OF CANADA, LTD
TORONTO

ATTENTION AND INTEREST

A STUDY IN PSYCHOLOGY AND EDUCATION

BY

FELIX ARNOLD, Ph.D.

𝔑𝔢𝔴 𝔜𝔬𝔯𝔨

THE MACMILLAN COMPANY

1910

Copyright 1910
By THE MACMILLAN COMPANY

Set up and electrotyped. Published February, 1910

THE MASON-HENRY PRESS
SYRACUSE, NEW YORK

Preface

The present essay on the psychology of attention and interest is an attempt to clarify and arrange the many facts that have been brought to light by numerous experiments in the psychological laboratories. I have felt myself bound, not to uphold any special theory or school, but to present the facts as they seem to be. The exposition of the subject under the categories, 'description,' 'illustration,' 'development,' 'explanation,' and 'definition,' is in line with the more modern and scientific presentation as seen in books on physiology, embryology, zoölogy, medicine, etc. Some may differ with me as regards the exact demarcation of the different aspects of the subject. The facts, however, are not changed because of any scheme of presentation. My chief obligations are to J. M. Baldwin, J. McKeen Cattell, E. L. Thorndike, E. B. Tichener, F. J. E. Woodbridge, and other exponents of the scientific attitude towards facts and the presentation of facts.

FELIX ARNOLD

New York City.

CONTENTS

PART III—EDUCATION

CHAPTER IX

CHAPTER X

INDEXES

PART I
ATTENTION

Part I
Attention

CHAPTER I

THE GIVEN SITUATION IN ATTENTION

§ I. DESCRIPTION

1. THE SUBJECT-OBJECT RELATION. In a loose and popular manner, the object, as different from the subject is readily recognised. The man who picks up a book to read, the woman who selects goods for a dress, the child who plays with the toy, each, in a vague way, distinguishes an object which exists apart from the self. There may be present no intensive analysis of the nature of such existence, or of the meaning of the relationship, but for the practical purposes of usage and experience, the object, as existing apart from the subject, has a more or less utilitarian or esthetic value. In scientific research and laboratory experimentation a more rigid interpretation of 'object' is made. Close analysis is necessary sharply to define exactly what is 'subject' and what 'object' in a given situation, and every effort is made to eliminate the personal equation, emotional bias, illusion, or other per-

sonal factors. The astronomer limits his field to a portion of the heavens, the botanist busies himself with a bud, a seed, a root fibre, .the geologist restricts his activity during a given investigation to some strata, rock formation, or what not, and so with investigators in other lines. Some situation is selected and treated as an object apart from the self. Many situations in the course of an investigation are so considered and made the object of close study.

The psychologist differs in nowise from other scientific investigators. In his work he deals with specific situations, and examines, interprets, analyses, and reasons much like scientists in other fields. His point of attack may be different, his interpretation may deal with qualitative or with quantitative aspects differing from those selected by a botanist or a physicist, but his basis is much like theirs. If his work is to have any value, it must be based on situations which have a concrete filling of some kind, on objects which are more or less definite, on situations which, while they are under investigation, must be considered apart from the self which is concerned with the experimentation. The scientific point of view is one which is recognised by the psychologist, but which is seldom held by cultured workers in other fields. The mind is usually considered by such as an ethereal will-o'-the-wisp, a spirit which appears, now here, now there, and which is so evanescent that one can speculate about it with safety, draw deductive conclusions, and construct hypotheses which can not be tested in concrete situations. That popular opinion is wrong in this connection will be readily understood by one who has seen the laboratory study of mental processes. Not the mind, but some situation is studied with special reference to consciousness. A given field is made the center of attention, tested according to some definite method, and studied in an inductive manner.

In general, the subject-object relation is one, which, from long habit, is accepted as a matter of course in most fields. This dual relationship fits in with the nature of things, stands the test of experience, of application, of work, and is believed in, regardless of metaphysical or other disquisitions to the contrary. From this point of view all else stands opposed to the self. Self and the rest of the universe constitute the whole. No doubt the rest of the universe exists for the self as an 'other' of related parts, as a whole which is affected by every act of the individual. In actual practice so extended an 'other' is nar-

rowed down to some definite situation which can
be manipulated and controlled. In a piece of
work, a laboratory experiment, for example, the
individual is not immediately concerned with the
rest of the universe. He may affect it, his actions
may result in a redistribution of relationships,
but this is no direct concern of his. He is usually
concerned with only what is under his immediate
control. The rest of the universe is not so much
'object,' as 'objective' to him. The object is
rather the point of junction between the individual and the rest of the system, between himself
and all that is 'objective.' Some limited portion
constitutes for the time the point of junction between the individual and what is objective. The
individual localises his efforts and restricts the
extent of his control.

2. THE POINT OF JUNCTION. 'Point of junction' corresponds loosely to what is called 'object,'
as, for example, the material in an experiment, a
place of business, a reading room in a library, a
tool, or what not. Different kinds of such objects, however, may be distinguished.

(a) *Real.* As one looks before one and con-
siders what one sees, the object in such a case is
visual and somewhat extended. If touch and
motor control enter in the determination of the

object, the field at once becomes extremely narrowed. If other senses are involved, the field receives a richer content and means more to the individual who is in control. The quality and the extent of the point of junction thus depend upon the senses which are involved in the experiences. Any sense may mediate a point of junction. We may have a visual field, an auditory or a tactile field. So, too, a situation may be determined by all together. Usually several of the senses are called into play. An object is seized, tested, taken apart, put under the microscope, and controlled in as many ways as possible.

What is before one at any moment, what exists as a single pulse of apprehension, therefore, can not always be said to constitute a situation given in full. To be given *in toto,* to have the feel of reality, a situation must allow of reactive adjustment, must be under some kind of motor control. Only as one is before a situation which can be manipulated and reconstructed in a practical way, only as one can test the visual field by active selection and adjustment, can it be considered as basic and real. An essential aspect of a basic situation is this impelling and necessary character which it receives through touch and motor control. It may be denied metaphysically, it may be doubted philosophically, but practically, doubt or denial means destruction. For example, tentative denial of a stone wall may result in a bruise or other injury. Scholastic disbelief must be swept aside when actual contact is effected. Contrariwise, belief is never so strong as when motor control reinforces visual apprehension.

The more direct and immediate control is possible when the situation is beneath one's feet or under one's hands. The various junctions, visual, auditory, tactile, etc., can then be bound together by the motor. Such a limited field is further widened by means which will facilitate motor contact. The microscope enlarges the visual field without bringing it outside of direct motor control, the railroad and the telegraph enable one to make as many points of contact as possible within a given time, touch and motor control are aided by delicate instruments, machinery does work which the hands can not do, and so on. Where no means exist for the realisation of motor control, a situation must remain incomplete, may, in fact, be considered a chimera. The pot of gold at the other end of the rainbow, for example, has still to be felt as a reality.

(b) *Ideal.* In an ideal, schematic, and representative sort of way a situation may assume a form somewhat removed from the original. An outline, plan, picture, word, image, idea, thought, may take the place of the situation for the individual, may, in a number of ways, stand for the actual situation. One who wishes to buy a book, for example, needs but to utter the necessary words in order to realise his intention. 'Book' in such a case is all that is necessary for the purpose. If it is to be read, however, it must exist in more real form.

When a situation is present in ideal form it receives the stamp of reality when it points to some foundation situation which can be directly controlled in a motor way. It receives a tinge of the impelling and necessary nature of foundation situations only by the feel of motor tendencies which impel realisation. A book which, when thought of, calls forth tendencies to open and touch it, is much more real than simply 'book' spelled out or seen only visually. So, too, the idea of a plaything has reality for the child when he feels tendencies to play with it. An ideal scheme can have reality only as affecting practice, only as it leads to some basic situation. Until such realisation is possible it must be incomplete, it must exist much like a visual situation which lies outside the field of direct motor control.

Even as partial, as schematic and formal, ideas and images assume for the time a form determined in part by foundation situations. As a formal object, the thought exists in the shape of a word, diagram, outline, or expression. The formal aspect of thought and ideation receives its stability by the same means which give stability to basic situations. Motor control is called into service for the purpose of fixing the formal elements of ideal situations. Speech, writing, drawing, illustration, construction, etc., give to images and ideas a form which enables them to receive further verification in application and practice. In ideal situations we can not readily escape motor control. Images which are so flitting and transitory as to be outside the bounds of motor control and definite realisation of some sort, practical or esthetic, must stand outside the pale of belief. As ideal situations they can have little value.

(c) *Possible.* Ideal situations which have arisen out of immediate experience and direct control naturally have the feel of reality to a greater degree than ideas or images which have been acquired in a more indirect way. If, for example, one has seen snow, felt it, and handled it, one will have a greater belief in its existence, will read a reality into the word 'snow' more readily than the savage who has simply heard of it. Much of what is given in instruction, in reading, in conversation, etc., has a reality only in an indirect manner. Upon the basis of whatever experience has been acquired, a number of ideal situations acquire a reality in terms of transferred control. One may not have seen an emu, but if one is told that it is a bird similar to the ostrich, one more readily gives the term a reality which can be tested in some immediate, concrete situation. So, too, one may never have been in China, but actual situations before one, ideal situations in the form of pictures, descriptions, and the like, give one a basis which may be transferred to the possible situation implied in the term 'China.' The situation is possible in that there is a certain belief in its existence, in possible control and reaction in a sensorimotor manner. One feels sure, for example, that China exists, that travel to it is possible, that certain reactions may take place in it, that control in it is much like that under present conditions.

The possible, it is seen, is a form of the ideal, but it is a form in which transferred motor coefficients are called into service to give backing to belief in what is considered possible. Often one will believe in the reality of a possible situation which to others is just as surely a chimera. The broader and deeper the foundation of experience, the stronger will be the belief in situations which, to the untrained mind, seem to have no reality. The situation, for example, which was a possible one for Columbus and the early navigators, did not excite the same belief in the people about him. It became, to some extent, a real situation, when actual control was realised.

§ II. ILLUSTRATION

1. REAL. Real situations are best illustrated by laboratory and similar experimentation. Several examples will be given.

ACTION OF CHLOROFORM AND ETHER. Excise two frogs' hearts and place each in a watch glass containing 5 cc. of Ringer's fluid. To one add one drop of pure chloroform and cover with another watch glass. The heart will become feeble, lose tone, and finally stop beating. It will take about ten times as much ether to produce the same effect. Chloroform is ten times more potent a drug than ether.[1]

Strike the chord c-e-g strongly upon the piano keyboard, directing the attention to the c. Is it intensified?

[1] *Practical Physiology*, by A. P. Beddard, L. Hill, J. S. Edkins, J. J. R. Mcleod, and M. S. Pembry, 75.

Strike the chord again, directing the attention to the *e* or *g*. Is the tone attended-to intensified?[2]

Take two pieces of the same green paper. Lay one on a red background, the other on a background of its own color. Cover as before (with very thin tissue paper) and compare the two greens. Do similarly with red on a green and on a red background.[3]

2. IDEAL. The two meanings of ideal should not be confused. In an ethical sense, 'ideal' refers to hope and aspiration, in a psychological sense, 'ideal' signifies simply what is representative, cognitive, imaginative, and the like.

1. Think of a bunch of white rose-buds, lying among fern leaves in a florist's box.

(a) Are the colours—the creamy white, the green, the shiny white—quite distinct and natural?

(b) Do you see the flowers in a good light? Is the image as bright as the objects would be if they lay on the table before you?

(c) Are the flowers and leaves and box well-defined and clear-cut? Can you see the whole group of objects together, or is one part distinctly outlined while the others are blurred?[4]

Etc., etc., etc.

As for the scheme I had in my head, it was not a bad one in itself. I was to go down the sandy spit that

---

[2] Titchener, Edward Bradford, *Experimental Psychology*, 1: Pt. I, 111.

[3] Thorndike, Edward L., *The Elements of Psychology*, 232.

[4] Titchener, E. B., *Exp. Psych.*, 1: Pt. I, 198.

divides the anchorage on the east from the open sea, find the white rock I had observed last evening and ascertain whether it was there or not that Ben Gunn had hidden his boat; a thing quite worth doing as I still believe.— *Treasure Island*, Stevenson.

Thou shalt not hate thy brother in thine heart: thou shalt in any wise rebuke thy neighbour, and not suffer sin upon him.

Thou shalt not avenge, nor bear any grudge against the children of thy people, but thou shalt love thy neighbour as thyself.—*Leviticus*, 19.

3. POSSIBLE. In a possible situation, realisation may be effected, or it may be simply hoped for. Both are illustrated in the following.

Macbeth.   My dearest love,
Duncan comes here to-night.
Lady Macbeth.   And when goes hence?
Macbeth.   To-morrow, as he purposes.
Lady Macbeth.   O, never
Shall sun that morrow see!

And there shall accompany them fair damsels having large black eyes; resembling pearls hidden in their shells: as a reward for that which they shall have wrought. They shall not hear therein any vain discourse, or any charge of sin; but only the salutation, Peace! Peace! And the companions of the right hand (how happy shall the companions of the right hand be!) shall have their abode among lote trees free from thorns, and trees of mauz loaded regularly with their produce from top to bottom; under an extended shade, near a flowing water,

and amidst fruits in abundance.—*The Koran*, Sura LVI,
Eng. tr. by G. Sale.

The last passage is a good illustration of transferred control. As Muir points out, Mohamet
painted a Paradise which would appeal to the
pleasure loving Arab, which 'would captivate the
inhabitant of the thirsty and sterile Mecca.' In
this case a basis of real experience was used in
the reconstruction of an ideal Paradise which
would be believed in by the Arab.[5]

4. ILLUSTRATION BY DIAGRAM.

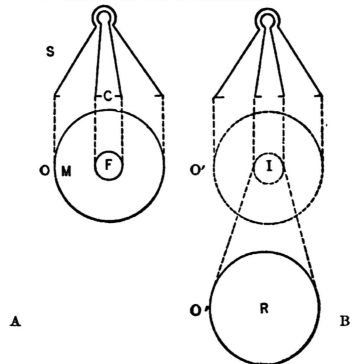

FIG. I. A, real. B, ideal. S, subject.
O, real object. O', ideal object. O",
situation to which the ideal refers.
F, focus. M, margin. O, center of
control.

[5] Muir, William, *The Life of Mohamet*, 75.

§ III. DEVELOPMENT

1. STAGES. It is highly probable, that the newly-born child is not conscious of subject or object in the same manner as is the grown adult. One is so accustomed to look upon an object as having some kind of existence apart from the subject that one tends to overlook the fact that this twofold relationship is the result of considerable development, the end station, as it were, of a somewhat complicated series of movements on the part of the child. Even in the developed consciousness, it is somewhat difficult sharply to differentiate what is subject, and what is object. In philosophy, for example, one aspect is often taken as basic, and the attempt is made to explain the other in terms of it. In psychology, too, one or the other aspect is unduly emphasised. As far as attention is concerned, from the objective side, it is viewed as simply a state of clearness and distinctness. From the subjective side, it is sometimes considered as ideal reinforcement or arrest of incoming impressions, or, by the older writers, as a species of mental activity.

It must be remembered, in the first place, that subject and object, though looked upon, in a developed state, as two distinct things, have existence only in a dynamic relationship, and, in the second place, that each in itself is an abstraction. We do not have the subject, as such, and apart from some connection with an object. So, too, an object, by itself, means nothing, as far as the conscious subject is concerned. An object is an object, only as it affects a subject, only as there is action and reaction of some sort between the two. In a state of attention, for example, the subject attends to some situation, and some situation is in the focus of attention. We speak of each in a logical manner as having a separate existence, but such discussion does not affect the situation as it actually exists. Continual treatment of these two phases, subjective and objective, as isolated units, leads one to look upon them as units which exist in independence of each other. In any conscious moment, however, the two will be found together.

In the first pulse of life there is probably neither self nor object as a distinct phase of a situation. There is probably in the newly-born consciousness an undifferentiated whole, in which neither subject nor object stands out as a distinct existential fact. The nearest state in the adult consciousness is the dreamy condition usually present just before one goes to sleep, or when one is half asleep, and half awake. Out of this

2

raw material are developed notions of self and object. In early childhood self and object are often confused, and the gross division between the two is the result of considerable development. When the object is looked upon as more or less distinct from the self, attention, though existing from the very beginning, can be considered as a separate, conscious process. The three stages may be illustrated by the following diagrams, each of which represents a phase of a complicated process which at times combines the other phases:

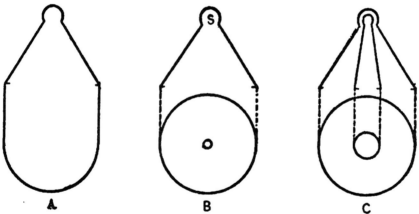

FIG. II. A, subject and object not differentiated. B, subject (S) and object (O). C, object in the focus of attention.

2. PROCESS. The process by which the notions of 'self' and 'object' are constructed is essentially a motor one. As soon as more or less definite motor reactions and movements begin, as in seizing and grasping, some portions of the field

of consciousness become outlined, cut out of their setting, and woven into the personal history of the individual concerned. A child which seizes a pencil, for example, plucks it out of its setting, gives it outline, uses it perhaps, and places it as a separate object among other objects. While the pencil may have had a more or less distinct visual outline, its control by the child would give greater vividness and strength to impressions of its separate existence. In fact, for grown people, manipulation and motor control is a test of the individual existence of an object. If one is not certain, for example, whether an object is fastened to some other, is part of it, or one separate from it, one will take it in hand, lift it, and try it in a number of ways.

The changing nature of the objective field, too, tends to give it the stamp of existence apart from the self. A portion of the field comes and goes, suffers reconstruction or even destruction, and seems a flux opposed to a more or less stable background of individual feeling and consciousness. It is the same mass of feeling, for instance, which accompanies the act of throwing a toy out of the window, as that which goes with the activity of looking out of the window, or of going down stairs to look for the toy. Feelings of

motor activity, of satisfaction, pain, etc., are referred to the self in a more or less conscious
manner. These give the self a value as a more
or less unchanging, existential fact. In addition,
visual elements, as of form of the body, remain
much the same, and reinforce the feelings of
motor activity, satisfaction, ease, quiescence,
pleasure, and the like.[6]

An aid in this process of differentiation is
such control of others as enters into the child's
field of experience. Conflict of control will
bring out the 'other' as a separate factor in the
total field. The difference in the conduct of
others when entering in the same field of objects
controlled by the child will also tend to stamp
the 'other' as an existential fact apart from objects within the child's field of activity. A grown
person, for example, will take an object from
the child, will take the child from the object,

[6] See: Stout, G. F., 'The Genesis of the Cognition of Physical
Reality,' *Mind,* 15, 1890. Baldwin, James Mark, *Mental Develop-
ment in the Child and the Race,* 112-120, and *Social and Ethical
Interpretations in Mental Development,* Ch. I. Preyer, W., *The
Development of the Intellect,* Eng. tr. by H. W. Brown, Ch. XIX.
Compayre, Gabriel, *Development of the Child in Later Infancy,*
Eng. tr. by M. E. Wilson, Ch. VIII. Wundt, Wilhelm, *Grundzüge
der Physiologischen Psychologie,* 3: Ch. XVIII, § 1, f. James,
William, *Principles of Psychology,* Ch. X. and *The Meaning of
Truth,* Marshall, H. R., *Consciousness,* Arnold, F., 'Conscious-
ness and its Object,' *Psych. Rev.,* 12, 1905.

will assist the child in the control of the object. Such conflict of control, even with adults, emphasises the existence of another as a separate fact which is to be reckoned with in the manipulation of objects.

Within the objective field many changes may take place because of the manipulation and control attempted by the child. Development of the situation may proceed by increase in the number and kinds of the points of contact which are made. When a child sees an object, he usually tries to seize it, bite it, throw it about, take it apart, test it in every possible manner. Each point of junction is a new experience for the child and gives fuller meaning to the situation in hand. Development of a situation is also possible through reconstruction or partial destruction. To a beholder the activity of the child may not mean development, may, in fact, seem a waste of time, or a positive nuisance. But to the child such control as he exercises, whether destructive or not, results in a widening of his own experiences, and in instructive changes in the field before him.

Successive acts of control result in increased differentiation and development. Residual effects accumulate both in the subject and in the

objective field.   In the individual such cumulative results are represented by habits, mental
dispositions, memories, and the like.   The child,
in popular parlance, 'will know better next time.'
In the objective field we have, in the more advanced stages, material progress, tradition, moral
law and order, custom, etc.   The latter then re-
acts on the former and tends to preserve control
within the grooves of custom.   The social background is usually able to enforce its conventions
and manners on the individual, who, in turn, may
be able to effect changes in such conventions and
traditions.   Action and reaction go together, here
as elsewhere.   On the basis of cumulative residua,
the individual is able 'to rise on his dead self
to higher things.'   Whatever he has accomplished
can be used as a foundation for further control.
The child, for example, who has mastered writing and reading, is able to spend his energy on
other things.   Below is a schematic outline which
illustrates progress and individual endeavour on
a broad platform of habit.

Development of a situation in the manner suggested above demands a narrowing of the field
under manipulation, a fixation of the object, a
closer and more refined series of adjustments, a
more delicate interpretation, a finer feel or body

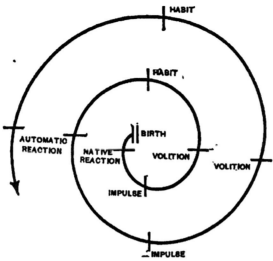

FIG. III.   Individual   Development   (after
Baldwin, J. M., *Ment. Dev.*).

attitude, in short, attention.   The subject must
select his object, examine aspects of it, try it
in various ways, and control it in a more or less
definite manner.   Self and object exist together,
each is influential in producing changes, each
must be considered in relation to the other.   The
objective side of the situation gives us the field
of attention.   The subjective side gives us those
motor adjustments, ideal elements, and reinforcing factors which are usually present in the more
advanced stages of attention.   Both aspects, the
subjective and the objective, must be considered
in the treatment of attention.

§ IV. EXPLANATION

Certain biological considerations necessitate
such differentiation and discrimination as are

found in the subject-object relation, and in attention. Some restriction of the objective field is necessary for the continued existence of the organism. Discrimination and selection are necessary even in animal life, and in the more elementary functions of eating and drinking. The savage who misses his aim may have to go hungry or starve. The hunter who can not find signs of water may perish. The child who is unable to control his knife will cut himself. The adult who does not hear the horn of the electric car may lose his life. Focalisation and definite reaction are necessary to ensure a modicum of ease and satisfaction. Strange and uncommon situations which may result in pain or death must be focalised before further reaction of definite nature is possible. Moreover, focalisation with selection may be needed to ensure safe control.

Where a situation is more or less known, further knowledge is possible only by analysis, discrimination, selection, and restricted control. Scientific workers are continually constructing mechanical aids by means of which given situations can be cut up into smaller parts, restricted within a limited field, and intensively controlled. Specialisation is but another name for such focalisation and concentration.

CHAPTER II

THE OBJECTIVE ASPECT OF ATTENTION

§ I. DESCRIPTION

1. CLEARNESS AND DISTINCTNESS. A striking characteristic of the field of attention is the change in the clearness and distinctness which results from the motor and ideal processes which are aroused. As control of a situation becomes restricted, as the field narrows and becomes cut out of its setting, it is said to become distinct. The situation is distinct in that it is more or less sharply defined, in that it stands out from its surroundings. The outline of a flying bird as seen against a clear sky, the blur on the horizon which is recognised as a ship, these are distinct, though they can not be said to be clear. When, in addition, the parts of the situation stand out within the whole, when the relations between the parts become evident, the situation is said to be clear. The flying bird is then seen to have certain coloration, the ship is then recognised as a steamship, with two or more stacks, and so on. Distinctness refers to the totality as set off against a marginal background. Clearness re-

fers to a further differentiation of the parts within the whole.

Clearness and distinctness are terms which have historical connections. Descartes used clearness and distinctness as signs by which to judge of the truth of notions.

I call that clear which is present and manifest to an attentive mind; . . . and distinct, that which is so separate and distinguished from every thing else that it contains within itself only that which is clear.[1]

Clearness and distinctness have also been em-emphasized in connection with visual metaphors. The *'Blickpunkt'* view of attention has been prominently brought forward by Wundt and Titchener, but it was used long before them. Fortlage likens attention to the 'clear glance of observation'[2] and Lotze compares it to the 'retina of the eye.'[3] Hamilton writes in a similar strain.

Consciousness may be compared to a telescope, attention to the pulling out or in of the tubes in accommodating the focus to the object; and we might, with equal justice, distinguish in the eye, the adjustment of the pupil from the general organ of vision, as, in the mind,

[1] *Princ.*, Pt. I, § XLV.
[2] Fortlage, Karl, *System der Psychologie*, 1855, § 12.
[3] Lotze, Rudolph Hermann, *Medicinische Psychologie*, 1852, § 37.

distinguish attention from consciousness as separate faculties.[4]

This predominance of visual terminology is not strange when we consider, as Jevons points out, that at least 246 words in the English language have been derived from the root 'spec.'[5]

A third characteristic of the field of attention, emphasised by some, denied by others, is intensity, or rather, increase in intensity. Considerable discussion of the hair-splitting variety may be found defending one or the other view.[6] Any contentions one way or the other in this connection disregard the basic function of such changes in the situation as take place. These changes are secondary and subordinate to the motor control and manipulation which is to be

---

[4] Hamilton, Sir William, *Lectures on Metaphysics*, Lect. XIII.

[5] See, Wundt, W., *Grund. d. Phys. Psych.*, 3:333-339. Jodl, Friedrich, *Lehrbuch der Psychologie*, 2:74. Titchener, E. B., *Exp. Psych.*, 1:Pt. II, 89, and Lectures on the Elementary Psychology of Feeling and Attention. Fraser, Alexander, 'Visualisation as a Chief Source of the Psychology of Hobbes, Locke, Berkeley, and Hume,' *Am. Jour. of Psych.*, 4:230-247.

[6] See: Stumpf, Carl, *Tonpsychologie*, 1:§ 4, 2:§ 22. James, W., *Princ. of Psych.*, 1:425. Kuelpe, Oswald, *Outlines of Psychology*, Eng. tr. by E. B. Titchener. Lough, James E., 'The Relations of Intensity to Duration of Stimulation in our Sensations of Sight,' *Psych. Rev.*, 3:484-492. Münsterberg, Hugo, and Kozaki, N., 'The Intensifying Effect of Attention,' *Psych. Rev.*, 1:39-44. Pillsbury, W., *Attention*, Ch. I. Titchener, E. B., *El. Psych. of Feeling and Attention*.

effected.   There is no inherent virtue in either
increase or decrease in intensity.   Such a change,
in itself, means little.   It is the purpose which
the change is to subserve which determines
whether or not there is to be an increase in the
intensity of incoming impressions.   If increase
of intensity will facilitate more perfect control,
then the individual will secure such increase in
intensity and illumination, by artificial means, if
necessary.   Usually, ideal and motor reinforcements are called into service to secure increase
in the intensity of an impression.   If one listens
closely enough, one may hear a sound which has
no real existence.   If ideal elements can not be
used, mechanical instruments are called into play.
On the other hand, if a more modified atmosphere
is necessary, a situation may be plucked out of a
too intense and blinding illumination, and placed
in one more subdued.   An artist will examine a
picture with half-closed eyes.   One may, in fact,
close one's eyes entirely to a too obtrusive situation.   Intensity may or may not be found according as control calls for it or not.   Increase
in intensity, when present, is possible only within
narrow limits.   One can, for example, follow a
diminuendo with increasing attention.   The resulting increase in intensity is only a relative one,

and does not of necessity force the notes to their maximal strength. The diminuendo will remain a diminuendo, but with a less steep descent.

2. PERSISTENCE. In attention, the situation becomes more or less distinct and clear. In addition, it may persist for a time in the focus of the given field. Such persistence depends in great measure upon the points of contact which can be made, and upon the ideal elements which can be excited. When an object allows of esthetic interpretation, motor control, etc., the probabilities are that it will hold attention longer than will a more barren object. So too, a field which revives numerous ideas and images, will stay in the focus for a considerable time. One who gazes long at a time-table does not do so solely because of any inherent interest in the printed matter before him.

The three characteristics, clearness, distinctness, and persistence, inhere in the objective field, in the situation under control. The tendency to treat consciousness as a special kind of activity has led some to speak of the clearness and distinctness of the mental state, of consciousness in general. Without a content, however, a mental state has no meaning. In attention to an object, the clearness is present in the given field. The object becomes more clear and distinct. It is not a more highly illuminated consciousness which is poured over a situation to brighten it up, but a control which makes more distinct and clear selected portions of the given field.

3. FLUCTUATION. When minimal visual impressions are fixated steadily for a time the impressions do not continue at a uniform intensity but undulate, as it were, in a kind of rhythm. One who gazes steadily at a grey ring on a white background, for example, will find that the ring becomes less distinct, then more distinct, then less distinct, and so on. The one ring will yield a fluctuating series of impression. Such moments of distinctness or indistinctness, *i.e.,* from distinctness to indistinctness, or from indistinctness to distinctness, vary from 5 to 25 seconds. It is to be noted that such fluctuation is evident with only very weak impressions.

Experimental investigation has shown a number of concomitant phenomena.

(1) Fluctuation is closely related to respiratory and vasomotor changes.

(2) Slight sensory stimulation increases the length of the periods in which the distinct waves

persist. More intense stimulation decreases them, *i.e.*, when the visual impression is very weak the distinct period is longer than when the impression is stronger.

(3) Fatigue decreases the length of the periods in which the distinct waves. persist.

(4) The fluctuations correspond with the diurnal periodicity of general vitality. The periods of greatest distinctness are usually longer in the morning than at evening.

(5) Pathological conditions affect the fluctuations of attention. Thus 10 g. of alcohol decrease the length of the periods of fluctuation and induce a general fatigue, while 3 g. of brom. natr. increase the length of the periods. So, too, pathological conditions of depression or of excitation respectively decrease or increase efficiency in this connection.[7]

[7] Among others, see Eckener, Hugo, 'Untersuchungen über die Schwankungen der Auffassung minimaler Sinnesreize,' *Phil. Stud.*, 8:343-387. Galloway, E. C., 'The Effect of Stimuli upon the Length of Traube-Hering Waves,' *Am. Jour. of Psych.*, 15:499-512. Hammer, Bertil, 'Zur experimentellen Kritik der Theorie der Aufmerksamkeitsschwankungen,' *Zeit. f. Psych.*, 37:363-376. Heinrich, W., und Chwistek, L., 'Ueber das periodische Verschwinden kleiner Punkte,' *Zeit. f. Psych.*, 41:59-73. Hylan, J. P., 'Fluctuations of Attention,' *Psych. Rev.*, 3:56-63. Lehmann, Alfred, 'Ueber die Beziehung zwischen Athmung und Aufmerksamkeit,' *Phil. Stud.*, 9:66-95. Marbe, Karl, 'Die Schwankungen der Gesichtsempfindungen,' *Phil. Stud.*, 8:615-637. Pace, Edward, 'Zur Frage der Schwankungen der Aufmerksamkeit nach Ver-

The following tables give in seconds the periods of distinct vision and indistinct vision, under normal conditions, and with accompanying stimulation from different sources. The attention in each case was fixated on a revolving disc having on it a circle of grey (Masson disc).[8]

SUBJECTS

	NORMAL			INDUCTION CURRENT			SMOKING		
	V	NV	T	V	NV	T	V	NV	T
Av. of 7 tests	6.0	4.9	10.9	4.5	4.5	9.0	7.1	4.2	11.3
				ETHER			BALSAM		
Single tests	6.7	6.7	13.4	5.0	5.4	10.4	3.3	4.1	7.44

V.=visible, *N.V.*=not visible, *T.*=total.

Induction current. A slight current was passed through the left hand while the subject was looking at the Masson disc.

Smoking. Subject smoked during the process of fixation.

Ether, balsam. Odors were smelled during the experiment.

TABLE I

suchen mit der Masson'sschem Scheibe,' *Phil. Stud.*, 8:388-402. Pillsbury, W. B., 'Attention Waves as a Means of Measuring Fatigue,' *Am. Jour. of Psych.*, 14:277-288. Seashore, C. E., 'Die Aufmerksamkeitsschwankungen,' *Zeit. f. Psych.*, 39:448-450. Slaughter, J. W., 'The Fluctuations of the Attention in some of their Psychological Relations,' *Am. Jour. of Psych.*, 12:313-334. Taylor, R. W., 'The Effect of Certain Stimuli upon the Attention Wave,' *Am. Jour. of Psych.*, 12:335-345. Wiersma, E., 'Untersuchungen über die sogenannten Aufmerksamkeitsschwankungen,' *Zeit. f. Psych.*, 26:168-200, 28:179-198, 31:110-126. For further references see Pillsbury, W. B., *Attention,* and Titchener, E. B., *The Psych. of Feeling and Attention.*

[9]From, Taylor, R. W., *Ibid.,* 337, 339.

SUBJECT E

	NORMAL			INDUCTION CURRENT			AFTER STIMULATION		
	V	NV	T	V	NV	T	V	NV	T
Av. of 4 tests	15.3	10.5	25.8	17.1	12.8	30.0			
				SUBJECT B					
Av. of 3 tests	5.6	2.5	8.1	6.6	2.5	9.1	5.4	2.8	8.2

TABLE II

Fluctuation in the case of minimal visual impressions seems to be well established. In the case of minimal auditory and tactile impressions, however, it is highly probable that any fluctuation similar to visual fluctuation does not take place. It is extremely difficult to establish any definite waves of distinctness and indistinctness in such cases. One should go through a series of tests before accepting a few results of somewhat doubtful experimentation. If sound is used, the stimulation must be minimal and persistent as far as the mechanical arrangements are concerned. Simple tones seem to remain constant, and very light weights (cork) on the hand give no evidence of fluctuation. This can be tried by any one.[9]

[9] See Titchener, E. B., *Feel. and Attent.*, 267, and *Am. Jour. of Psych.*, 10:95.

3

4. UNITY. Before one discusses the unity of attention one should state exactly what one refers to by such unity and also what conditions hold when such unity is tested. For example, it is true that one can recognise a word as easily as one can a letter. The unity is then the word as a whole and not the separate letters which compose the word. So, too, one can glance at a page and give the number of words on the page as two or three hundred. What is then in the focus of attention is the single page which means or signifies the number of words. It would hardly hold, however, that three hundred words, as separate words, were seen in the one act of apprehension. It is usually held that in the visual field attention to four or five distinct and separate objects is possible.[10] If these objects are really seen as separate objects, then the statement is true, that attention is possible to five objects. But if through long association and habitual motor adjustments, certain groupings have come to mean 'five,' if contact and manipulation of objects have shown such objects to be five, and to stand for 'five,' then the single act of attention to groupings of four or five would result in the recall of 'five' as a number whole associated with

[10] See, for example, Pillsbury, W. B., *Attention*, Ch. VI.

the group. In such a case, even though 'five' means a series, a number of successive acts of counting, a succession of distinct and separate events, the act of attention at the given moment did not necessarily include such counts or series. We look, for example, at a series of lines and cognise five at a given moment. Now do we actually see five distinct and separate objects at a glance, or do we recognise a group which experience has taught us is 'five,' and then interpret the 'five' another way, *i.e.*, as a series?

Two varying conditions lead one to believe that the latter is the case. When the length of time in which a group is exposed to an observer is shortened, fewer objects are seen in a single act of attention. So, too, the results differ when the ages of the observers differ. Griffing tested the pupils of the different school years with a series of letters. The observers looked at the fixation point, and at the signal, 'Ready,' the letters were shown for a given time. In the following tables are given the results of two series of tests, the first with a time limit of 1 second, the second with a time limit of .1 second.[11] A study of the figures will show the variation due to decrease in the time of exposure.

[11] Griffing, Harold, 'On the Development of Visual Perception and Attention,' *Am. Jour. of Psych.*, 7:227-236.

AVERAGE TOTAL NUMBER SEEN WITH 1 SECOND EXPOSURE FOR
DIFFERENT CLASSES

N	C	S	M V	R	M V	Max.	Min.	$\frac{R}{S}$
19	I	20	7	17	5	36	7	.85
17	II	30	5	26	4	38	20	.87
10	III	37	5	33	5	49	20	.89
20	IV	35	5	28	6	48	14	.77
15	V	40	7	36	6	43	25	.90
22	VI	44	6	38	5	54	28	.82
13	VII	51	8	44	8	58	29	.86
11	VIII	50	8	47	7	59	31	.94
10	High	59	2	55	6	60	40	.93

In this and the following table,

N.=number of pupils in the class.

C.=class by year.

S.=average of the total number of letters as seen in ten trials, six letters being given in each trial. The first, for example, 20, is the number seen in ten trials. This will give, for the first year, 2 seen in a single act of attention.

M.V.=mean variation of S.

R.=average of the total number seen correctly during the ten trials.

M.V.=mean variation of R.

MAX.=maximum of the total number seen by any individual during the ten trials.

MIN.=minimum seen correctly by any individual

TABLE III

AVERAGE TOTAL NUMBER SEEN WITH .1 SECOND EXPOSURE

N	C	S	M V	R	M V	Max.	Min.	$\frac{R}{S}$
22	I	8	6	3	3	17	0	.4
16	II-III	13	8	6	4	19	0	.4
12	IV	16	6	7	3	13	1	.4
17	V	18	5	14	4	22	3	.8
17	VI	22	10	12	5	25	0	.5
23	VII	19	7	14	5	23	0	.7
23	VIII	25	7	21	6	37	8	.8
84	High	30	5	23	6	47	4	.8
75	Coll.	32	6	29	6	59	11	.9

TABLE IV

It is seen that when the time of exposure was reduced from one second to one tenth of a second, the number of letters seen in a single act of attention dropped considerably, in most cases to less than half as many. It is also seen that the younger pupils were able to grasp a much smaller number of letters in a single act of apprehension than were the older ones. One can not say, therefore, that attention to five objects is possible, if one means five separate and distinct objects. All the pupils were shown the same letters, but such letters did not signify the same number wholes to the different pupils. As a simple, mechanical act, the seeing and the attention were the same in each case. The difference in the results was due to the difference in the development and training of the pupils, to the difference in the associations, and in the experience with numbered or grouped objects.

A series of experiments by Hylan show practically the same thing, namely, that the elements of time and experience are conditioning factors in the apprehension of groups of objects. In these tests six letters on each of twenty cards were exposed in succession, one letter at a time. The series of six letters was exposed for 20 σ. or 3.6 σ. for each letter. In the first tests, the shutter passed from right to left, and in the second from left to right. A signal was given before the exposure of the series. Each of the twenty cards was shown five times, this making one hundred exposures for each subject. The subjects gave both the letters seen, and their order. The results in the following table give the totals for the hundred tests.[12]

SUBJECT	A	H	R	S	V	Av.
No. seen correctly	212	222	158	160	224	195
No. seen wrong	40	30	58	50	58	47
No. misplaced	17	16	5	18	23	16
(Reversed)						
No. seen correctly	208	225	151	151	229	196
No. seen wrong	32	22	53	53	52	45
No. misplaced	6	13	10	10	9	9

TABLE V

The first effect of the letters was that of a single complex impression, some characters appearing distinctly outlined, some confused, and some entirely unseen. This conscious impression followed the exposure in much the same way that a positive after image follows a stimulation of light. It was sometimes possible to hold this impression with all its details an appreciable length of time without recognising a single letter, until each character was recognised one at a time. But it was more

[12] Hylan, J. P., 'The Distribution of Attention,' *Psych. Rev.*, 10:373-403, and 498-533.

frequent that one or sometimes two letters were recognised without being preceded by an appreciable interval, and these followed by one or two more, one at a time and in distinct succession.[18]

Hylan conducted a further series of experiments to test the distribution of attention and to find whether or not the groups are seen as groups of distinct objects, or as groups which are later analysed into their separate parts. Lines, numerals, letters, and words were shown on cards. Twelve cards were used five times each in each series. The smallest number of lines on a card was 4 (2 mm. apart), of numerals and letters, 3, and of words, 2. The observer was asked to give the arrangement of the single elements of an impression. The results in the following table are the totals of sixty tests. The per cent is that of the number of wrong cases seen. The time exposure was one tenth of a second.

Objects Exposed	Lines			Figures			Letters			Words		
	R	W	%	R	W	%	R	W	%	R	W	%
2										48	32	67
3				65	5	8	61	9	14	14	46	329
4	50	10	10	52	18	35	50	30	60	19	21	111
5	41	34	34	68	42	62	36	64	178	1	19	1900
6	41	34	34	31	59	190	14	46	329			

TABLE VI

[18] *Ibid.*, 398.

It is seen that attention is not evenly distributed over the given field, that it does not grasp a totality as a group of distinct objects, that, in fact, the number, five, six, etc., is due, either to an association of the group with the number, or an interpretation of the group, an analysis which has no place in the original act of attention. One can not, therefore, say that visual attention to five or six objects is possible. It is highly probable that attention to more than one or two distinct and separate objects is impossible. In fact, in attention to a number of series of three letters each, Cron and Kraepelin found that the middle letter was read correctly the most, the last letter a less, and the first letter the least number of times.[14] This would hardly be if there were such a thing as a single pulse of attention which grasped in detail several distinct objects.

Tests on attention to a succession of sounds show that as many as 8 can be apprehended as a group, and that when the sounds are so grouped, as many as from 2 to 5 groups can be

[14] Cron, Ludwig, and Kraepelin, Emil, 'Ueber die Messung der Auffassungsfähigkeit,' *Psych. Arbeiten*, 2:219. See also, Finzi, Jacopo, 'Zur Untersuchung der Auffassungsfähigkeit und Merkfähigkeit,' *Psych. Arb.* 3:289-384. Kleinknecht, H., 'The Interference of Optical Stimuli,' *Harvard Psychological Studies*, 2:299-308.

seized and retained. The most favorable time of succession in such cases seems to vary between 0.3 and 0.18 seconds.[15] As in visual impressions, so in auditory, it is highly probable that the sounds are not cognised as distinct and separate impressions, but rather as a group or rhythm which is connected with the number 'eight,' or which, as a rhythmic impression, comes to mean 'eight.' There still remains to be made a series of experiments in which a number of simultaneous auditory impressions are given with varying periods of persistence, as in the case of visual impressions.

In the field of touch Krohn gave simultaneous touch impressions to different parts of the body. He found that when the impressions were scattered, as many as six or seven could be apprehended as distinct and separate.[16] But as Hylan remarks, "It should be said, however, that after-images of touch were very persistent, and were used to a considerable extent in locating the sensations."[17] What has been said in connection

[15] Dietze, Georg, 'Untersuchung über den Umfang aes Bewusstseins bei regelmässig auf einander folgenden Schalleindrucken,' *Phil. Stud.*, 2:362-393, 384.

[16] Krohn, W. O., 'An Experimental Study of Simultaneous Stimulations of the Sense of Touch,' *Journ. of Nerv. and Ment. Diseases*, 1893.

[17] Hylan, *Ibid.*, 378.

with visual impressions may therefore be considered to hold in the case of touch sensations. In visual, auditory, and tactile attention, we may safely say that the number of objects to which one can attend is not more than one or two. Larger numbers must be considered as due to group associations, or to later analyses which interpret the group impression and read into it the different objects.

The different experiments have been made in visual, auditory, and tactile fields. Attention in the visual field is something different from attention in the auditory field, and the same is true of attention in the tactile sphere. We can not be said to possess any distinct and separate power of attention. Each field is distinct and separate. Just how many fields can be attended to at once, depends in part upon the connection of such fields with some common situation, in part upon the unity of motor control, and in part upon the experience of the subject. There is still to be performed a series of experiments which will determine just to what extent these conditions affect the unity of attention. Tests on distraction shed considerable light on the subject. As these will be considered under the topic of facilitation and arrest, they need not be discussed here. From the data thus far presented, however, it seems safe to infer that what we have is not a single pulse of consciousness, not a uniform field of attention, but rather a number of concomitant pulses of consciousness, a number of synchronous situations. In most cases the visual and the motor coalesce, but this need not always be so. When visual, motor, or other fields coincide in a single situation, unity is usually possible in the field of attention. When such fields, however, inhere in different objects, when stimulation comes through different channels and from different objects, partial attention to each may be possible, depending upon the complexity of the situation and the intensity of the attempted control. In short, we have a number of attentions, and not a single power of attention. This, however, is anticipating later discussion.

5. FACILITATION AND ARREST. Under the name of 'distraction of attention' a number of experiments have been made with a view of determining the effects of extraneous stimulation on attention to some given fields. Some of these tests showed that at times the results were better when the so-called distraction was attempted. For example, when music was played on a piano while the observer lifted weights and discrimi-

nated them, the results were better than when there was no music.[18] Such tests, however, are based on the assumption that error alone is the means of detecting distraction of attention. These tests, too, assume that extraneous stimulation is one of the few means of securing distraction. A great deal of experimentation in various fields, however, has shown that attention may be arrested or facilitated in a number of ways, and that such facilitation or arrest is made evident by means other than error in the results. One aspect which must be considered in detecting facilitation or arrest is *time*. If, under the new conditions, the results are secured in less time, attention may be said to be facilitated. If more time is required, attention may be said to be arrested. If the time remains constant, then facilitation is shown if there are less errors in the results, and arrest is shown if there are more errors in the results. A second aspect of importance is the *number* of objects which can be attended to as objects within a given time, and under the new conditions. If more objects can be cognised under the new conditions, then attention is facilitated, if less, attention is

[18] Talbot, E. B., 'A Study of Certain Methods of Distracting the Attention,' *Am. Jour. of Psych.*, 9:332-345, and 336, 344. See also Moyer, F. E., *Ibid.*, 8:405-413, and Birch, L. G., *Ibid.*, 9:44-55.

arrested. When the time remains constant, then increase in the complexity of the given field will result in more errors if attention is arrested, and less, if attention is facilitated. The third means of showing facilitation or arrest is the number of *errors* which results. If the time remains constant, and the given field remains constant, then arrest is shown if the new conditions produce more errors, and facilitation is shown if they give rise to less errors. The conditions under which facilitation or arrest may be produced will be considered in the following sections. It is seen that extraneous stimulation is only one of a number.

(*a*) *Simplicity versus complexity.* Of the two given fields, the one which is more complex will hold attention a longer time. This is shown by the following test, in which, for each series of 100 fluctuations in attention to the simple figure,

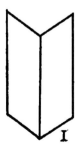 

FIG. IV.

there were less for the complex figure. The following table gives the exact ratios.[19]

Observer	A	B	C	D	E
Figure I	100	100	100	100	100
Figure II	50	70	35	35	20

TABLE VII

In Hylan's tables, the same is shown by the test of error. When the time remained constant, and the observer was asked to give the arrangement of each of the parts of the given field, the wrong cases averaged 34 per cent when the field consisted of five lines, 62 per cent when it contained five numerals, 178 per cent for five letters, and 1900 per cent for five words. When the number of objects was four instead of five, the per cents were, for lines, 10 per cent, for numerals 35 per cent, for letters 60 per cent, and for words 111 per cent. The time exposure in these tests was one tenth of a second.[20] Cattell found that it took much longer to recognise and name a color or a picture, than it did a letter or a word. The following table is of interest both for psy-

[19] Gordon, Kate, 'Attention as Determined by the Complexity of the Presented Content,' *Psych. Rev.*, 10:278-283.

[20] See above, page 39, table VI.

chological and pedagogical reasons. The time is given in thousandths of a second.[21]

Letter		Word		Word		Color		Picture	
A	476	Bond	405	Baum	423	Blue	515	Anchor	535
B	413	Cause	428	Berg	417	Green	532	Eye	503
C	424	Chair	411	Bild	424	Red	559	Tree	517
D	411	Child	411	Brief	440	Black	505	Hatchet	513
E	424	Death	405	Buch	443	Yellow	575	Image	574
F	420	Earth	406	Ding	435	Rose	578	Leaf	567
G	426	Fact	385	Fluss	424	Violet	611	Flower	586
H	422	Faith	379	Form	409	Grey	697	Fish	487
I	451	Force	373	Gold	450	Brown	608	Bottle	561
J	415	Head	362	Haus	403	Orange	730	Glass	596
K	409	House	388	Jahr	454			Hand	490
L	423	King	408	Kind	450			Hat	446
M	422	Life	424	Kunst	461			Can	600
N	422	Light	414	Land	441			Cross	591
O	409	Love	404	Licht	441			Light	552
P	393	Mind	418	Mann	439			Moon	587
Q	418	Name	410	Nacht	447			Scissors	558
R	446	Plan	396	Recht	445			Boat	486
S	410	Ship	390	Stadt	449			Umbrella	556
T	409	Slave	402	Stern	432			Shoe	493
U	441	Song	389	Theil	424			Key	560
V	423	Style	442	Tisch	449			Star	498
W	432	Time	408	Traum	454			Chair	534
X	412	Truth	424	Volk	428			Table	547
Y	463	World	408	Welt	445			Watch	562
Z	421	Year	412	Zahl	469			Bird	566
Ave.	424		404		438		591		541
M.V.	17		14		14		38		25

TABLE VIII

In the case of the colors an added factor in the arrest of attention was the difficulty in finding

[21] Cattell, James McKeen, 'Ueber die Zeit der Erkennung und Benennung von Schriftzeichen, Bildern, und Farben,' *Phil. Stud.*, 2:635-650, and 'Psychometrische Untersuchungen,' *Ibid.*, 3:304-335, and 452-492. The latter is the most important and contains the table given.

the right name for the color. It is to be noted
·that with the words, the totality as a whole was
named. There was no attempt to discriminate
or arrange the letters of the word.

(b) *Pleasure-pain.* The general effects of
pleasurable or painful situations are well known.
A field which is pleasing to the individual tends
to hold the attention, one which is painful, to
repel the attention. In smelling odors, some
pleasant, some unpleasant, 19 students reacted
either by relaxing the hands and letting the
head drop back (extension), or by contracting
the hands and letting the head drop forward.
The following table gives the number of cases:

REACTIONS	UNPLEASANT		PLEASANT		INDIFFERENT	
	Cases	Per Cent.	Cases	Per Cent.	Cases	Per Cent.
Flexion	240	66.6	118	32.2	15	49
Extension	120	33.3	248	67.8	16	51
Ratio	2 : 1		1 : 2+		1 : 1	

TABLE IX

The experimenters make this additional note:

Other tendencies are present, however, such for example as the tendency to move towards an object which
attracts attention; the tendency to move away from a

disagreeable object; the tendency to make particular movements of adaptation to stimuli; etc.[22]

Lloyd Morgan's experiments with animals show the same thing.

To some other chicks I threw cinnabar larvae, distasteful caterpillars conspicuous by alternate rings of black and golden-yellow. They were seized at once, but dropped uninjured; the chicks wiped their bills—a sign of distaste—and seldom touched the caterpillars a second time. The cinnabar larvae were then removed, and thrown in again towards the close of the day. Some of the chicks tried them once, but they were soon left. The next day the birds were given brown loopers and green cabbage-moth caterpillars. These were approached with some suspicion, but presently one chick ran off with a looper, and was followed by others, one of which stole and ate it. In a few minutes all the caterpillars were cleared off.[23]

Attention may be attracted by a situation which excites feeling, but the persistence of such attention is determined in part by the pleasure-pain elements which enter. One can, of course, attend to a situation in spite of the pain which exists, but, other things remaining the same, at-

[22] Dearborn, G. V., and Spindler, F. N., 'Involuntary Motor Reaction to Pleasant and Unpleasant Stimuli,' *Psych. Rev.,* 4:461, 462.

[23] Morgan, C. Lloyd, *Habit and Instinct,* 41.

4

tention will tend to persist when the situation is pleasurable, and to lag when it is painful.

When pleasure-pain elements are present in a situation, they tend to impel attention. The strength of the shock is dependent upon the suddenness and the intensity of the impressions which impel consciousness. In order of their stimulating efficacy are situations which produce (1) profound emotions, (2) violent affective conditions, (3) transitory and superficial emotions, unexpected impressions, intense impressions, (4) continuous sensations, and (5) quiet mental application under favorable conditions. On the other hand, the stability and regularity of attention are conditioned by situations which produce the above changes in reverse order.[24]

(c) *Quality of the impression.* When an impression is more intense, it produces a greater shock and stimulates attention more than when it is weaker. Angell and Thompson found that of two noises, when both were unexpected, 'a loud noise produced a much more violent shift of attention than a slight one.'[25] A strong stimulus will produce the same effect as a weak one in

[24] Angell, James Rowland, and Thompson, Helen Bradford, 'A Study of the Relations between Certain Organic Processes and Consciousness,' *Psych. Rev.*, 6:32-69.

[25] *Ibid.*, 62.

half the time, that is, attention is more readily aroused by the more intense impression. As Lough shows,

> A strong stimulus acting for half the time necessary to produce its maximum effect gives rise to a sensation of exactly the same intensity as that produced by half as strong a stimulus producing its maximum effect.[26]

Differences between black and white are much more quickly perceived when the sensations are more intense. As the differences between the shades become smaller, i.e., as the impressions become weaker, the time necessary to discriminate them becomes longer. Intensity of impression may therefore be considered as a facilitating influence as far as the impelling of attention is concerned.[27]

An impression, too weak in itself to excite attention, will finally succeed in stimulating attention if repeated. This phenomenon is known as 'summation of stimuli.' A succession of weak impressions then has the force of one more intense stimulus.

[26] Lough, James E., 'The Relations of Intensity to Duration of Stimulation in our Sensations of Light,' *Psych. Rev.*, 3:484–492.

[27] Cattell, J. McKeen, 'The Time of Perception as a Measure of Differences in Intensity,' *Phil. Stud.*, 19:63–68, Henmon, V. A. C., 'The Time of Perception as a Measure of Differences in Sensations,' *Arch. of Phil., Psch., and Sci. Meth.*, 8.

(d) *Time*. When more time is allowed during
an act of attention, facilitation results, when less
time is given, arrest follows. In Griffing's tests,
a decided fall was shown in the number of letters
seen, when the exposure was reduced from one
second to one tenth of a second, and a still
greater fall was evident in the number seen correctly. Arrest is here shown both by the decrease in the number seen, and by the increase in
the errors.[28] The tests of Cron and Kraepelin
show a similar decrease in the number of right
cases seen when the time of exposure is decreased.
With apertures respectively 5 mm., 4 mm., and
3 mm., the corresponding time exposures were
290 σ, 230 σ, and 170 σ, (σ equals a thousandth
of a second). When syllables were shown
through these openings, more wrong cases occurred with the shorter exposures, as is shown
by the following table:[29]

PER CENTS. OF RIGHT CASES SEEN

SPACE IN MM.	5 M M.	4 M M.	3 M M.
Time in %	100	79.3	58.6
Right cases in %	100	97.0	87.7

TABLE X

[28] See above, page 36, tables III and IV.
[29] Cron, L., und Kraepelin, E., 'Ueber die Messung der Auffassungsfähigkeit,' *Psych. Arb.*, 2:203-325.

(e) *Age.* The experiments conducted by Griffing show that the older the child who attends, the better will be the results of his attention, both in the number of letters seen in the given moment, and in the accuracy of these results. When six letters were exposed for one tenth of a second, and the observers asked to write down what they saw, the older pupils were able to record a greater number and a more accuate result as is shown by the following table:

N	Age	S	R	M.V.	Max.	Min.	$\frac{R}{S}$
39	7-9	11	$4 \pm .4$	3	33	0	.4
77	10-12	20	$13 \pm .3$	3	32	0	.6
73	13-15	24	$18 \pm .6$	6	37	0	.7
132	16+ (18)	32	$27 \pm .4$	6	59	8	.8

N.=number tested,

S.=average of the total number of letters written down as seen in ten trials, six letters being shown in each trial,

R.=average of the total number seen correctly,

Max.=maximum of the total number seen by any individual,

Min.=minimum of the total number seen correctly by any individual.

Probable errors of the values of R. are given in the R. column preceded by the sign $+$.[20]

TABLE XI

Messmer found that adults take less time to read the ordinary printed page than do children, and

[20] Griffing, Harold, 'On the Development of Visual Perception and Attention,' *Am. Jour. of Psych.,* 7:230.

that children of older age excel those who are younger. Thus an adult will take 200-500 σ to read a word or letter at a normal rate of speed, a child of 11 years of age, 300-700 , one of 9, 400-800 σ, and one of 7, 500-1000 σ, as the table below shows:[31]

Age	7				9				11				Adult			
Direct	Forw.		Back		Forw.		Back		Forw.		Back		Forw.		Back	
Letter	R	G	R	G	R	G	R	G	R	G	R	G	R	G	R	G
N. Wd.	775	770	990	952	415	460	585	645	375	420	565	600	297	305	467	465
F. Wd.	632	750	785	950	380	425	500	577	305	337	495	575	295	290	370	395
F. Let.	585	750	775	810	460	465	590	555	410	410	525	472	270	310	372	360

Direction, forward or backward,
Letters, Roman or Gothic,
N.Wd., words read at a normal rate of speed,
F.Wd., words read fast,
F.Let., letters read fast.
Results are in thousandths of a second, and are the averages of 100 words or letters read.

TABLE XII

(f) *Preadjustment.* When an observer expects a stimulus, and gets ready to react to it, attention is usually facilitated. When the impression is unexpected and when the observer is not ready to receive it, attention is usually

[31] Messmer, Oskar, 'Zur Psychologie des Lesens bei Kindern und Erwachsenen,' *Arch. f. d. Ges. Psych.*, 2:190-298.

arrested. In general, preadjustment of the sense organs and body attitude is favorable to attention. Dwelshauvers made a series of experiments in which the subject reacted to a stimulus with a signal and without a signal. When no signal preceded the stimulus the reaction time was greatly lengthened. In the table below the signal preceded the stimulus at periods of 1½, 3, and 6 seconds. The results are given in thousandths of a second.

Sig. Interval	1½ seconds		3 seconds		6 seconds	
	S	M	S	M		
Signal	257.02	129.78	279.66	133.22	299.86	144.8
No Signal	308.6	184.	304.03	183.45	301.97	196.97

S. attention concentrated on the stimulus,
M. attention concentrated on the reaction.
When no signal was given the intervals of stimulation were respectively 30, 45, and 60 seconds.[32]

TABLE XIII

In simple reactions to sound with no signal, with irregular signals, and with regular signals, Martius obtained the following results:[33]

[32] Dwelshauvers, Georg, 'Untersuchungen zur Mechanik der activen Aufmerksamkeit,' *Phil. Stud.*, 6:217-249.
[33] Martius, Götz, 'Ueber die muskuläre Reaction und die Aufmerksamkeit,' *Phil. Stud.*, 6:167-216.

SIGNAL	S	M
None	198.4 186.2	161.9 172.5
Irregular	108.0 144.8 151.7 171.0	87.4 120.8 123.3 155.7
Regular, 1 second interval	123.4 122.0 144.6 157.0	118.1 109.0 134.0 143.3

TABLE **XIV**

Cattell also found that when the time between the signal and the stimulus was delayed and varied up to 15 seconds, the reaction time was lengthened.[34]

(g) *Reinforcement.* Ideal preparation facilitates attention especially when the image or idea corresponds to some aspect in the given situation. In a series of tests Münsterberg showed this conclusively. He used 400 pictures 5 times each, thus giving 2,000 exposures. Two seconds before he showed a picture to the observer he called out a word. The picture was then shown and the subject was asked to tell what he saw. Of the 2,000

[34] Cattell, James McKeen, 'Psychometrische Untersuchungen,' *Phil. Stud.*, 3:333.

cases, 617, or more than a third, were directly influenced by the word called out. The subject was not supposed to look for the object in the picture, in fact did not know that there was such an object as the word represented. In almost all of the other cases the picture was seen as a whole, or several objects in the picture were seen at once. In the 617 cases, on the other hand, a single object in the picture was distinctly seen.[35] The effect of ideal reinforcement is very manifest in individuals who see 'ghosts,' and in whom imagination overrides objective presentations. Ideal reinforcement also plays an important part in holding some topic in the focus of attention. In such cases associations are revived which enable some aspect of the field to persist in the field of clearness and distinctness.

(*h*) *Practice*. Practice facilitates attention, lack of practice arrests it. One who has had sufficient practice in a given field can attend more easily, more accurately, and more rapidly. In continuous work the effects of practice are lessened in part by the increasing fatigue. After a rest, however, the effects of practice are shown by the higher level of the results. In memorising

[35] Münsterberg, Hugo, *Experimentellen Psychologie*, Heft 4:12-17.

12 place figures for five quarters of an hour on four successive days Weygandt obtained the following results:

¼ hour	First day	Third day
1	197	680
2	269	636
3	250	663
4	310	541
5	238	415

TABLE XV

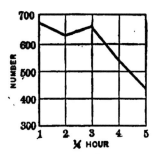

CURVE I. Effects of fatigue due to continued work. (See table XV, Third day.)

The results for the first quarter of an hour on each of the four successive days is given in the table below.

First	Second	Third	Fourth
197	360	680	864

TABLE XVI

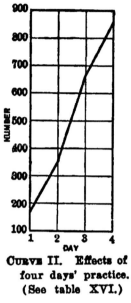

Curve II. Effects of
four days' practice.
(See table XVI.)

The number of figures memorised in each quarter of an hour are given. The curves based on these tables show the effects of fatigue in one day, and the effects of practice on the work of the succeeding day.[36] The marking of the letter 'i' in a text for five successive quarter hours on four successive days yielded similar results.

¼ Hour	First Day	Third Day
1	12424	14566
2	8176	13809
3	5612	7560
4	6157	7508
5	8876	7514

TABLE XVII

[36] Weygandt, Wilhelm, 'Ueber den Einfluss des Arbeitswechsels auf fortlaufende geistige Arbeit,' *Psych Arb.*, 2:118-202.

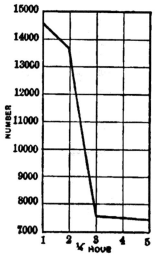

CURVE III. Effects of
fatigue due to continued
work. (See table XVII,
Third day.)

FIRST DAY	SECOND DAY	THIRD DAY	FOURTH DAY
12424	13876	14566	16078

TABLE XVIII

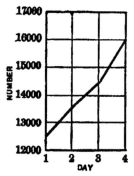

CURVE IV. Effects
of four days' prac-
tice. (See table
XVIII.)

When the activity is more or less new the rise
in the curve may be somewhat steep. A level is
finally reached much below or above which the
curve does not go. The effect of the practice is
then at its best. In reading Hungarian text for
five quarter hour periods for 24 successive days
(with one day's intermission on the thirteenth
day), Weygandt obtained the following results
for the first quarter of an hour on each day. The
results give the number of syllables read.

1	2	3	4	5	6	7	8	9	10	11	12
2724	2716	2793	2989	3027	2959	3102	2803	3314	2966	2968	3186

14	15	16	17	18	19	20	21	22	23	24	25
3320	3212	3367	3368	3585	3513	3656	3433	3604	3512	3507	3542

TABLE XIX

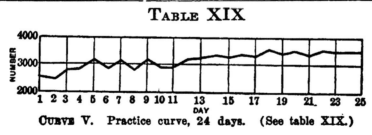

CURVE V. Practice curve, 24 days. (See table XIX.)

(*i*) *Fatigue.* Fatigue arrests attention. In
continuous work, the effects of fatigue are in
part interfered with by the effects of practice.
The downward drop in the curves given above
shows the effects of fatigue produced by the

work itself. One who is in a fatigued condition similarly does less effective work in new fields. An interesting series of experiments was carried on by Bettmann. He produced a state of fatigue in two ways, first, by one hour's continuous addition, and second, by a two hours' tramp. Work done while in a fatigued condition was then compared with similar work done under normal condition. The results are indicated below.[37]

SIMPLE REACTION WITH CHOICE

N		M		B	
σ	E%	σ	E%	σ	E%
290	2.7	403	1.3	264	24.
291	1.7	346	0.7	288	21.
300	3.3	395	1.0	221	35.
294	2.6	381	1.0	257	26.9

N.=normal, M.=mental fatigue, B.=bodily fatigue, σ = thousandth of a second, E%=errors.

TABLE XX

MEMORISING 12 PLACE FIGURES IN ONE HALF HOUR

	1	2	3	4	5	6	7	8	9	10	11	12	13	Ave.
N	468		564			613			709			761		661
M		474			413			478			528			476
B				405			401			506			518	454

TABLE XXI

[37] Bettmann, Siegfried, 'Ueber die Beeinflussung einfacher psychischer Vorgänge durch körperliche und geistige Arbeit,' Psych. Arb., 1:152-208.

ADDITION FOR ONE HALF HOUR

	1	2	3	4	5	6	7	8	9	10	11	12	13
N	1662		1782			1788			1961			1773	
M		1462			1532			1531			1753		
B				1502			1487			1591			1704

TABLE **XXII**

SYLLABLES READ IN ONE HALF HOUR (2 PERIODS ¼ HOUR, I, II)

	1		2		3		4		5		6	
	I	II	I	II	I	II	I	II	I	II	I	II
N			8484	8137					8757	9812		
M					7270	6961					8072	8338
B	8410	8294					8528	8288				

TABLE **XXIII**

In the last test the mental fatigue was produced by one half hour's addition, and the bodily fatigue by one half hour's walking. The effects of fatigue in these tests is shown (1) by a decrease in reaction time, (2) by an increase in error, (3) by a decrease in the number memorised, and (4) by an arrest of the effects of practice. The following curves show the effects of practice under normal conditions and the arrest of such effects in a condition of fatigue. The curves are based on the memory tests.

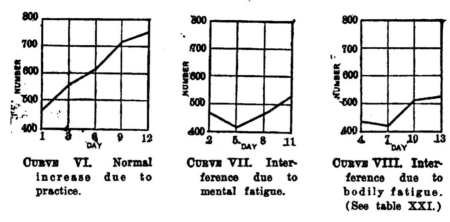

CURVE VI. Normal increase due to practice.

CURVE VII. Interference due to mental fatigue.

CURVE VIII. Interference due to bodily fatigue. (See table XXI.)

The following curve connects the effects of the successive tests and shows the drop due to fatigue and the rise due to normal conditions.

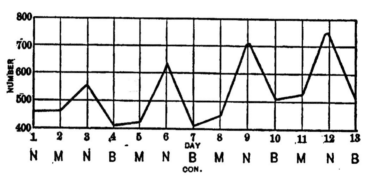

CURVE IX. Effects of mental (M) and bodily (B) fatigue on the normal (N). (See table XXI.)

(*j*) *Pause.* Under some conditions, pause with rest is favorable to the work immediately following, under other conditions it is unfavorable. During continuous work, the impulse to work gradually decreases, while the fatigue gradually increases. A pause with rest should then come when the impulse to continue the work is weak, and while the effects of fatigue are strongly in evidence. If, however, the impulse to work is strong and the fatigue is not great, a pause may be unfavorable to good results. The length of the pause, too, affects the work immediately following. If the pause is too long the effects of practice may be greatly diminished, and the impulse to work may become very weak. If the pause is too short the impulse may be interfered with and the effects of fatigue may still be strong enough to hinder further effort.[38] A number of experiments show that (1) a 5 min. pause at the end of a half hour's work is favorable, (2) a 15 min. pause under the same conditions is unfavorable, (3) a 15 min. pause at the end of an hour's work is favorable, (4) a pause of over a day is unfavorable.[39] The general effects of pause with rest are (1) passing away of fatigue, (2) weakening of the impulse to work, and (8) decrease in the effects of practice.[40]

[38] Heümann, Gustav, 'Ueber die Beziehungen zwischen Arbeitsdauer und Pausenwirkung,' Psych. Arb., 4:538-602.

[39] Amberg, Emil, 'Ueber den Einfluss von Arbeitspausen auf die geistige Leistungsfähigkeit,' Psych. Arb., 1:300-377.

[40] Lindley, Ernest, 'Ueber Arbeit und Ruhe,' Psych. Arb., 3:482-535. See also Rivers, W. H. R., und Kraepelin, Emil, 'Ueber Ermüdung und Erholung,' Psych. Arb., 1:627-678. Hylan, John P., und Kraepelin, Emil, 'Ueber die Wirkung kurzer Arbeitszeiten,' Psych. Arb., 4:454-494.

5

When the pause is filled with a different kind of work the effect on a continuation of the original work depends upon the kind and the difficulty of the work interpolated. If the interpolated work is of a difficult nature it may interfere with the work following. Thus, if memory work is interpolated between periods of less difficult work, the periods following the interpolated work show a decided fall in the results. The following tables and curves give some indication of the effect of such interpolated work.

ADDITION. INTERPOLATED WORK (HEAVY FACE TYPE) MEMORISING
OF NONSENSE SYLLABLES

¼ hr.	1 day	2 day	3 day	4 day
1	809	867	860	836
2	912	913	879	883
3	801	**144**	755	**146**
4	707	**142**	722	**126**
5	638	678	775	687

TABLE XXIV

Addition was of continuous one-place figures. Work of each day was divided into quarter-hour periods. Effect of the interpolation is shown in the fifth quarter-hour periods of the second and fourth days.[41]

[41] Weygandt, Wilhelm, 'Ueber den Einfluss des Arbeitswechsels auf fortlaufende geistige Arbeit,' *Psych. Arb.*, 2:118-202.

ADDITION. INTERPOLATED WORK (HEAVY FACE TYPE) MEMORISING OF 12-PLACE FIGURES

¼ hr.	1 day	2 day	3 day	4 day
1	800	929	867	958
2	812	839	920	947
3	792	**934**	823	**804**
4	763	**792**	783	**888**
5	707	638	757	671

TABLE XXV

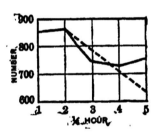

CURVE X. Effect of the interpolation of difficult work. Dash line shows the drop in the last period. (See table XXIV, 3 and 4 days.)

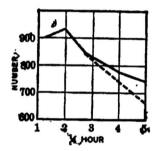

CURVE XI. Effect of the interpolation of difficult work. Dash line shows the drop in the last period. (See table XXV, 3 and 4 days.)

When the interpolated work is less difficult, the effect on the work following may be beneficial. The following tables and curves show this.

MEMORISING OF FIGURES. INTERPOLATED WORK (HEAVY FACE TYPE) ADDITION

¼ hr.	1 day	2 day	8 day	4 day
1	197	360	680	864
2	269	395	636	780
3	250	**698**	663	**745**
4	310	**662**	541	**689**
5	238	408	415	672

TABLE XXVI

MEMORISING OF NONSENSE SYLLABLES. INTERPOLATED WORK, SLOW WRITING

¼ hr.	1 day	2 day	8 day	4 day
1	128	101	128	120
2	88	91	116	122
3	86	**136**	120	**155**
4	80	**137**	88	**155**
5	59	111	88	145

TABLE XXVII

The change in the kind of work is beneficial even if such interpolated work is difficult in itself. This is shown in the above table, and more conclusively in the one following.

MARKING A LETTER. INTERPOLATED WORK, MEMORISING OF FIGURES

¼ hr.	1 day	2 day	3 day	4 day
1	15556	14890	16122	14473
2	18281	8514	12456	11882
3	14343	942	7832	1008
4	7918	942	7355	1056
5	9546	10684	6987	16322

TABLE XXVIII

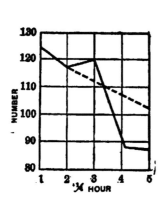

CURVE XII. Effect of the interpolation of easy work. Dash line shows the rise in the last period. (See table XXVII.)

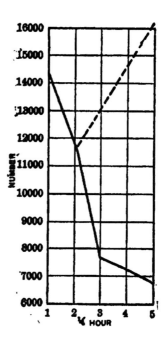

CURVE XIII. Effect of the interpolation of different work. Dash line shows the rise in the last period. (See table XXVIII.)

The interpolated work, memorising of figures, is so different from the basic work, marking a letter in a text, that the interpolation acts almost like a pause with rest. We may say that interpolated work acts favorably, (1) when it is different in kind from the basic work, and (2) when it is less difficult. It acts unfavorably, (1) when it is the same in kind, and (2) when it is more difficult.[42]

(k) *Hunger.* A most interesting series of tests was made by Weygandt to establish the effects of hunger on mental work. He went without food for periods of 12, 24, 36, 48, and 72 hours, and while in this condition went through a number of experiments. The results of his tests showed (1) that simple apprehension of syllables and words was not hindered to any great extent, (2) that association time was not influenced much, (3) that memorising was arrested, (4) that distraction had a greater arresting power, and (5) that reaction with choice gave a larger number of errors. The results of some of his work are given below.[43]

---

[42] *Ibid.*, 123, 133, 136, 139, 142, 144, 147, 152, 155, 157, 161, 168, 190.

[43] Weygandt, Wilhelm, 'Ueber die Beeinflussung geistiger Leistungen durch Hungern,' *Psych. Arb.*, 4:45-173.

MEMORISING OF NONSENSE SYLLABLES (12 IN A GROUP)

Day	1	2	2	3	3	4	4	5	5	6	6	7	7	8	8	9	9	10
Time	E	M	E	M	E	M	E	M	E	M	E	M	E	M	E	M	E	M
Con.	N	N	12	24	(N)	N	N	N	12	24	36	48	(N)	N	F	N	N	N
15min.	149	136	108	87	176	250	226	322	206	208	137	137	181	218	176	285	324	396
15min.	142	133	100	92	177	233	266	290	189	144	151	92	154	214	120	293	262	356
30min.	291	269	208	179	353	483	492	612	395	352	288	229	335	432	296	578	586	752

N=normal, 12, etc.,=hunger for 12 hours, etc., F=mental fatigue, E=evening, M=morning, (N)=normal period immediately following a period of hunger.

TABLE XXIX

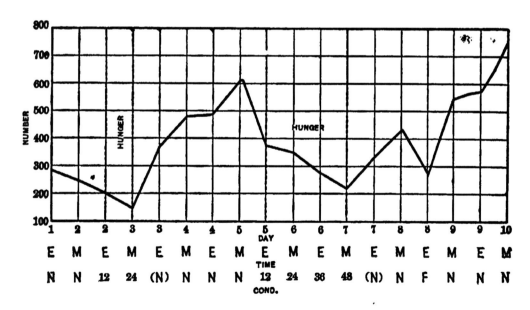

CURVE XIV. Effects of hunger. E, evening. M, morning. N, normal, 12, 24, etc., hunger for 12, 24, etc., hours, (N), normal period after hunger. F, mental fatigue. (See table XXIX.)

(l) Obstructed breathing. By means of a nostril plug, Kafemann produced interference with breathing similar to that caused by adenoids. The obstruction in the breathing produced a decrease in the efficiency of the work attempted. In the addition of figures the following results were secured:

ADDITION FOR ONE-QUARTER HOUR PERIODS WITH AND WITHOUT OBSTRUCTION

	Normal	Normal				Normal
1 day	1306	1324	1256	1249	1246	1323
	Normal	Obstructed				Normal
2 day	1334	1213	1223	1189	1184	1276
	Normal	Normal				Normal
8 day	1493	1447	1430	1399	1363	1381
	Normal	Obstructed				Normal
4 day	1453	1362	1356	1340	1366	1421

TABLE XXX

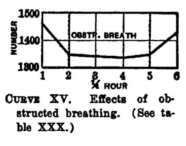

CURVE XV. Effects of obstructed breathing. (See table XXX.)

On the second and fourth days, a quarter-hour's addition under normal conditions was followed by an hour's addition with obstructed breathing, and this was followed by another quarter-hour's addition under normal conditions.[44]

(*m*) *Weak mindedness.* In general, weak mindedness, when compared with the normal, shows itself in (1) increase in error in the apprehension of syllables and words, (2) increase in reaction time, and (3) decrease in the amount of work done. Reis tested six paralytics (P), eight hebephreniacs, (H), and two normal subjects, (N) with the following results.

APPREHENSION OF NONSENSE SYLLABLES

	10 mm.			5 mm.		
	R	W	O	R	W	O
N	96.94	2.86	0.19	93.90	5.73	0.37
H	77.97	11.40	10.63	61.10	20.08	18.82
P	69.45	28.82	1.73	57.98	35.85	6.17

ONE-SYLLABLE WORDS

	R	W	O	R	W	O
N	96.25	3.48	0.27	97.25	2.74	0.
H	84.56	5.88	9.59	71.19	9.50	19.31
P	74.44	18.30	7.36	52.86	14.01	29.76

Exposure of 10 mm. gave a time of 670 σ, one of 5 mm. gave a time of 335 σ.

R=number of right cases, W=number of wrong cases, O=number omitted.

TABLE XXXI

[44] Kafemann, Rudolf, 'Ueber die Beeinflussung geistiger Leistungen durch Behinderung der Nasenathmung,' *Psych. Arb.*, 4:435-453.

REACTION TIMES

	N		H		P	
.	Time	%	Time	%	Time	%
Color	549	100	720	131.2	756	137.7
Letter	627	100	709	113.1	807	128.9
Word	554	100	697	125.2	799	144.1
Addition	1071	100	1243	115.1	1442	134.6
Judgment I	931	100	1074	115.6	1434	154.0
Judgment II	862	100	1103	127.3	1308	150.7

The time is given in sigmas, or thousandths of a second.

Recognition of a color, letter, and word was timed.

Addition of two numbers between 1 and 19 was required.

Judgment I. Subject was required to tell which of two classes, 'living' or 'dead,' a one-syllable word described.

Judgment II. Subject was asked whether the word excited a pleasant or an unpleasant feeling.

TABLE XXXII

ADDITION OF 7+7, ETC., IN 1 MINUTE

N	H	P
32.2	29.2	30.9

ADDITION OF 12+12, ETC., IN 1 MINUTE

25.9	22.6	22.3

TABLE XXXIII

The afflicted subjects showed greater fatigue and less practice effects. The paralytics were least efficient in this respect.[45]

(n) *Extraneous stimulation.* When two activities are in the same field or in related fields, one will tend to arrest the other. Vogt recited a poem orally, and at the same time added single figures without writing down the answers. He found some difficulty in retaining the sums in his memory. Interference was also felt with the muscular-acoustic images of the sums, and there was eye-strain due to an effort to visualise the sums. During the first day only oral·rendition of the poem was attempted. On the second and third days addition of figures was included during the second half hour of the work. The ratios of the number of syllables recited with and without interference is given in the last column. The results of the tests are as follows.[46]

[45] Reis, Joseph, 'Ueber einfache psychologische Versuche an Gesunden und Geisteskranken,' *Psych. Arb.*, 2:587-694. See also Cron, Ludwig, und Kraepelin, Emil, 'Ueber die Messung der Auffassungsfähigkeit,' *Psych. Arb.*, 2:203-325.
[46] Vogt, Ragnar, 'Ueber Ablenbarkeit und Gewohnungfähigkeit,' *Psych. Stud.*, 3:62-201.

Oral Recitation With Addition

	I(X)	I(X)	II(X)	II(X)	III	I:II::100
1	1325	1227	1269	1215	1180	95.5
2	1574	1502	596	530	1104	36.7
3	1595	1467	680	620	1362	42.5

Table XXXIV

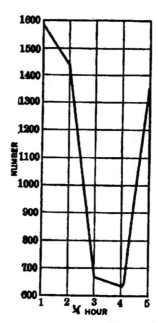

Curve XVI. Effects of
extraneous stimulation.
(See table XXXIV.)

Another series of tests included reading and writing, separately and together. In the following table, the first column gives the number of letters written in five minutes, the second the number of syllables spoken in five minutes, and the third the number of letters written, together with the number of syllables read while the writing was going on. The ratios are given in the last columns.

READING WITH WRITING

Day	W	R	W + R	W:W::100:	R:R::100:
1	857	3502	570+1739	66.5	48.6
2	878	3740	753+2273	85.9	60.9
3	903	3693	786+2280	87.0	61.7
4	926	3788	828+2459	89.4	64.9
5	941	3872	904+2679	96.1	69.2

TABLE XXXV

It is to be noted that during the third periods, more work was done, but each was somewhat arrested. In crossing out letters Vogt found that he made more errors and marked less letters with a text having meaning than with nonsense words. The meaning of the text acted as an arresting influence.[47]

When stimulation is in two fields not closely related, excitation in the one may facilitate attention in the other. Darlington and Talbot found that while music was played on a piano during the lifting of weights, there was better discrimination than when no music was played. So, too,

[47] See also Kleinknecht, H., 'The Interference of Optical Stimuli,' *Harvard Psychological Studies*, 2:299-308.

Moyer concludes from a series of experiments that visualisation of colors, hearing of sounds made by falling balls, and the smelling of odors are not arrested by such processes as adding, writing, and the like. In these tests the criterion of arrest was error. There was no record of time. Some arrest may have occurred in the increase of time due to the added activity. Even though there were no more errors in the tests, there might have been an increase in the time needed to discriminate the weights, recognise the odors, add, etc.[48]

In retinal rivalry, one figure in the stereoscope may be considered as an influence which arrests the other. When the figure has some content it tends to hold the field longer than one which is empty, i.e., to arrest the simpler figure for a longer time. Breese recorded the time during which each of a number of figures held the attention. His results are given in the table below.[49]

[48] Darlington, L., and Talbot, E. B., 'Distraction by Musical Sounds,' Am. Jour. of Psych., 9:332-345. Moyer, F. E., 'Addition and Cognate Exercises: Discrimination of Odors,' Ibid., 8:405-413. Birch, L. G., 'Distraction by Odors,' Ibid., 9:44-55. Swift, E. J., 'Disturbance of the Attention during Simple Mental Processes,' Ibid., 5:1-19.

[49] Breese, B. B., 'On Inhibition,' Psych. Rev., Mon. Sup., 3:1-65.

Experiments	Red, per cent of times seen	Green, per cent of times seen	No. of changes for each field
1	30	70	19
2	32	68	27
3	27	73	18
4	28	72	23
5	21	79	21
6	36	64	20
7	27	73	21
8	30	70	21
9	34	66	19
10	23	77	22
11	24	76	20
12	43	57	25
13	42	58	25
14	45	55	33
15	50	50	27
16	57	43	22
17	59	41	29
18	52	48	21
19	52	48	24
20	39	61	26
21	40	60	31
22	53	47	25
23	49	51	27

TABLE XXXVI

In experiments 3, 4, 7, 8, 10, 11, 14, 15, 18, 19, 22, and 23, the fields were reversed.

§ II. ILLUSTRATION

1. CLEARNESS, DISTINCTNESS, PERSISTENCE.

(a) *Literary.*

It was such a crowded scene, and there were so many objects to attract attention, that at first Nicholas stared about him, really without seeing anything at all. By degrees, however, the place resolved itself into a bare and dirty room with a couple of windows, whereof a tenth part might be of glass, the remainder being stopped up with old copybooks and paper. There were a couple of old rickety desks, cut and notched, and inked and damaged, in every possible way; two or three forms, a detached desk for Squeers, and another for his assistant. The ceiling was supported like that of a barn, by cross beams and rafters, and the walls were so stained and discoloured, that it was impossible to tell whether they had ever been touched with paint or whitewash.—*Nicholas Nickleby*, Dickens.

Suddenly I perceive on my right, not far from me, a large dark object which I had not noticed before, and which is lightly and noiselessly approaching my ambush and the watering-place. Without a halt the dark, mighty mass comes nearer and still nearer. Now I can plainly see that there are two objects, one in front of the other. They stand opposite me, not more than one hundred and fifty paces off. They are rhinoceroses, full-grown ones, coming here to drink. How gigantic they look by moonlight!—*Flashlights in the Jungle*, C. G. Schillings.

(b) *Experimental.*

Look for the 'man in the moon.' Note the process of differentiation, selection, etc.

Follow some instrument in an orchestra. Compare its sound with that of the other instruments.

Strike the chord *c-e-g* strongly upon the piano key-board, directing the attention to the *c*. Is it intensified? Strike the chord again, directing the attention to the *e* or *g*. Is the tone attended-to intensified?[50]

2. FLUCTUATION.

Rotate a white disc similar to the illustration below. Fixate the faintest grey ring. Observe the fluctuations in intensity.[51]

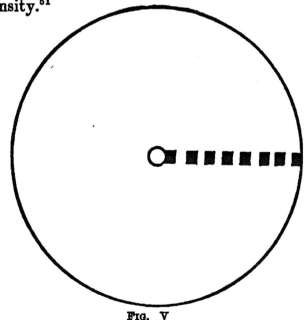

FIG. V

[50] Titchener, E. B., *Experimental Psychology*, 1:Pt. I, 111.
[51] Myers, C. S., *A Text-Book of Experimental Psychology*, 415.

6

Fixate some point on *be* in the following figure. What is the appearance of the figure? Move the eye slowly from *b* to *e*, and back again. Does the figure change in perspective? Move the eye from *b* to *c*, and back again. Is there any change? Fixate any point on line *be*. Note whether the line is in front of or behind line *ac*.[52]

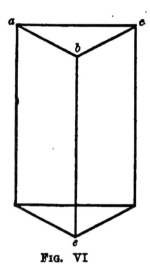

Fig. VI

Select a piece of cork which can barely be felt when resting on the back of the hand. Note whether or not there is any fluctuation in the pressure.

3. UNITY.

Look at each of the following groups of lines. Is there any difference when you look at them as a group, (a two-group, or a three-group, or a four-group), and when you look at them as two, three, or four individual lines?

[52] Titchener, E. B., *Ibid.*, 154.

FIG. VII

Look at the following series of lines. Is there any grouping? Note the different groupings.

FIG. VIII

Fixate the figure below. Note the different units which shape themselves. Are the elements of each group seen as a group or as individuals? Look at the dots in each group separately. Look at them as a group. What is the difference between the two acts of attention?[58]

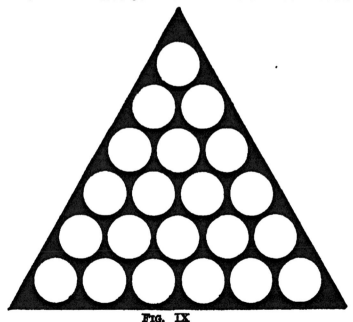

FIG. IX

[58] McDougall, W., 'The Physiological Factors of the Attention Process,' III, Mind, N. S., 12:487.

Read a page visually (silent reading), and note the time. Read the same page visually, attending to the letters and not to the words. Note the time. Note the difference in the groupings. Are the words seen as single words or as aggregations of separate letters?

4. FACILITATION AND ARREST.

With proper laboratory equipment, any of the experiments described in the preceding section can be repeated. For purposes of illustration, simpler ones can be tried.

(a) *Simplicity versus complexity.*

Place two figures in a stereoscope, one simple, one complex. Note the difference in the time in which each holds the attention. (The figures used by Breese are good. See above, Table XXVI).

Why does it take longer to read the words of a page, than to read the letters of the same page?

(b) *Time.*

Read the words of a page and note the time. Try to read two pages within the same time. What will be the result?

Mark all the *a*'s in a text for a period of fifteen minutes. Try to mark the same number in eight minutes. Note the result, with reference to (1) number of letters marked, (2) number of errors, (3) number of letters skipped.

(c) *Age.*

Let children of different ages read for five minutes.

Count the number of syllables read by each child and compare these numbers with the ages of the children.

Repeat Griffing's tests.

(d) *Preadjustment.*

Let children add single figures read out to them, with signal, and without. (Some signal, as 'Ready,' or 'Attention,' may be used.) Give such sums with (1) regular signals, (2) irregular signals, (3) no signals and irregularly or suddenly. Note the difference in the results.

(e) *Reinforcement.*

Repeat Münsterberg's experiment.

(f) *Practice.*

Mark *a*'s for fifteen minutes in the morning and fifteen minutes in the afternoon of each of ten successive days. Compare the numbers marked and plot the corresponding curve. On the eleventh day, read some text and note the appearance of the *a* as compared with the other letters.

(g) *Fatigue.*

Mark *a*'s for an hour or an hour and a half, and note the number marked every five or ten minutes. Plot the corresponding curve.

Produce fatigue by an hour's continuous addition, and read for half an hour. Count the number of syllables read. Read for half an hour at the same time on the next day when not fatigued. Compare the results. Mark letters for half an hour under similar conditions. Memorise poetry. Produce fatigue by a two-hours' tramp, and repeat the experiments. Compare the results.

(*h*) *Pause*.

Mark *a*'s for two hours. On the following day repeat the test, but rest for five minutes at the end of each half hour. Compare the results. Vary the periods of pause and the periods of work. Add figures, memorise nonsense syllables, etc., under similar conditions.

Mark *a*'s half an hour, read for half an hour, mark *a*'s again, and follow with half an hour's reading, in continuous periods of half an hour each for a period of two and a half hours. Make the periods of work and rest fifteen minutes each. Compare the results with those obtained in marking *a*'s for two and a half hours without the interpolated reading. Use a day for each experiment. Alternate marking *a*'s with marking *e*'s, with memorising, with continuous addition, etc. Use any of these occupations as basic, and interpolate any other. Note which facilitate and which arrest the basic work.

(*i*) *Extraneous stimulation*.

Read some passage visually for one minute, and at the same time repeat the multiplication table of 7's. Note the time which it takes to repeat each separately. Compare the resulting times.

Write a passage from a book and at the same time multiply the numbers from 5 on, by 13 for three minutes. Note the time necessary to do each separately. Is the total time greater or less than three minutes?

Repeat Vogt's experiments.

(*j*) *General*.

Test underweight children, overweight children, backward children, defective children, etc. Let them cross out letters for a given period, add columns of figures, divide, write, read, etc., and note (1) the time, (2) the amount of work done, and (3) the errors.

§ III. DEVELOPMENT

The general change in a field under fixation is from indistinctness to distinctness and from obscureness to clearness. In attention to any totality, the dim background gradually falls away and leaves the situation clear and distinct. Further manipulation and control results in a differentiation of parts, in greater systematisation and order, in an increase of clearness. The process, in short, is from discreteness to unity.

In the passage from childhood to adolescence, and then to adult life, there is an increase in the grasp of attention at any given moment, and a greater ability to hold attention for a longer period of time. The tests of Griffing show the development in the grasp of attention and Messmer's tests in reading indicate a similar development. As children grow older they are able to grasp more at a given moment, and to do this within less time.

§ IV. EXPLANATION

1. BIOLOGICAL. Reaction, adjustment and control are not effective vitally unless there is a

more or less distinct field before the organism. The essential aspect of a situation, the stimulating part of the field, the pleasure-pain feature of an environment must be singled out and selected if the individual is to persist as an individual. On this account every part of the organism strains to further the production of distinctness in the essential aspect of any background. The bull-dog jumps for his enemy's throat. The deer turns his head towards a light, or a noise. Failure in selection may mean death. The surgeon who marks the place where he is to operate, and carefully removes tissue, avoids blood vessels, and inserts a forceps or a knife, is an example emphasising the same thing.

In social and economic control, progress in any field is similarly the result of selection and specialisation. A situation is first dealt with in a more or less general way, differentiation is gradually effected, and then, piece by piece, the situation is attacked, analysed, studied, reconstructed, and again united in a more highly developed form. The development of factories, branch stores, special departments, offices, agents, etc., is characteristic of present-day life.

2. PSYCHOLOGICAL. (a) *Clearness, distinctness, and persistence.* The distinctness, etc., of

a situation is due to two sets of influences, (1) objective, and (2) subjective. Some of the more important of the objective conditions which give rise to clearness and distinctness are (1) difference, (2) change, (3) pleasure-pain, and (4) time. An impression differing greatly from those concomitant with it will tend to attract attention. The effects of difference in the intensity of impressions has been experimentally shown.[54] Common observation points to the same. A loud noise, a sudden report, a straw hat in winter, a cooling breeze on a hot day, the note of a piccolo or the clang of a triangle in an orchestra, these attract the attention. Change or variety also tends to stimulate and hold the attention. An object which is more complex may cause the attention to persist for a longer time. A simpler object may be more readily cognised, but its holding powers are not so strong. Pleasure-pain excites attention as already indicated in the preceding section. Finally, when more time is allowed, the development of clearness and distinctness are facilitated.

Of the more important subjective factors which facilitate clearness, distinctness, and persistence are (1) preadjustment, (2) reinforce-

[54] See above, page 50.

ment, (3) practice, (4) pause (rest), (5) age, and (6) natural vitality and mental ability. When one expects an impression and is ready to receive it, the organs, muscles, etc., are set in a certain direction. There is less waste in reaction and the field does not become blurred or indistinct through wrong or inadequate adjustments. When there is ideal reinforcement, the incoming impression is received by a disposition or system of images or ideas. By association, the impression is enabled to persist in the series of images or ideas revived. Attention to a time-table is an example of such persistence. Practice facilitates attention in that there is little waste. The situation and the organism fit each other. The organic set of the individual corresponds so closely to the different aspects of the situation, that the latter is enabled to flash into the focus of consciousness at once. Rest allows all the other factors to operate in their full strength. An older individual is better able to attend since his wider experience is accountable for more perfect practice, more highly organised mental dispositions and systems, and a more economical distribution of energy.

(b) *Fluctuation*. By considerable experimentation, the following facts have been ascertained in connection with physiological changes:

(1) Blood pressure sinks with every inspiration and rises with every expiration, though such concomitance is not exactly synchronous.

(2) Several such movements are contained in a larger rhythm, the so-called Traube-Hering wave.[55]

(3) Sensory stimulation tends to affect respiration and increase the length of the Traube-Hering waves.

(4) Fatigue, as evidenced by diurnal changes, tends to shorten the Traube-Hering waves.

(5) Pathological conditions, either natural (abnormal depression) or artificial (stimulation by alcohol), tend to shorten the Traube-Hering waves and to induce fatigue.

These vasomotor rhythms are controlled by a system of vasomotor nerves which have their centre in the cervical region and which control constriction and dilation of the blood vessels. The rhythmic rise and fall of blood pressure is measured by the rhythm in the rise and fall of the volume of the arm or finger.

By laboratory tests the following facts have

[55] *American Text-Book of Physiology*, 1:201. Howell, William H., *A Text-Book of Physiology*, Ch. XXXII.

been ascertained with reference to fluctuation of attention to minimal stimuli:

(1) Fluctuations of attention have a rhythm in which periods of brightest vision, for example, are succeeded by periods of dimmer vision.

(2) These waves correspond closely to Traube-Hering waves, and approximately with changes in respiration.

(3) Sensory stimulation tends to increase the periods of distinctness and illumination while increasing the length of the Traube-Hering waves.

(4) Fatigue, as evidenced by diurnal changes, tends to decrease the periods of distinctness and illumination, while decreasing the length of the Traube-Hering waves.

(5) Pathological conditions affect the rhythm of fluctuation as they do the rhythm of the Traube-Hering waves.

In attention to minimal impressions, the fluctuations are in all probability conditioned by vasomotor and respiratory changes. In part, fatigue of end organs and fluctuation of muscles of accommodation operate in causing fluctuation. In attention which is conditioned in part by accommodations of end organs and by ideal reinforcement, fluctuation does not exist in a pure state. In such a case it may be controlled in part by ideal and motor elements. This may happen in the case of retinal rivalry or in attention to such complex figures as Schroder's stair figure or Necker's cube.

In fluctuation, the changes in vasomotor action and respiration are normal physiological changes which condition attention to minimal stimuli and affect the periodicity of efficiency as shown in the fluctuations. It should be noted that such changes are not the ones which result when active control of a situation is attempted. Changes which follow active control and attention are the result of attention in such a case and not the conditioning substratum. Fluctuation of attention is a most interesting problem for in it we have attention in its purest state and as close to a general power in a sensory field as can be found. In a more advanced stage, attention is conditioned by acquired ideal and motor elements which further persistence, and guide attention one way or the other. Individual instincts and capacities also direct attention into special fields. It might be of interest to see whether or not persistence in any special field can be measured by the length of the periods of distinctness in fluctuation waves, and by Traube-Hering rhythms.

(c) *Unity.* Since efficiency of control is

facilitated by narrowing and specialising a given field, unity will tend to be selected in preference to distribution of attention. Moreover, complete control is possible only when a given totality is presented as a unitary whole. We have but a single body with which to take an attitude, a single pair of hands with which to work and manipulate an object or situation. The visual field, too, holds objects together in an elliptical form which may become further narrowed in motor control. Finally, when too many objects strive to hold the focus of attention, there results a feeling of strain, of unrest, of dissatisfaction, even of pain. On this account there will be a tendency to shut out such disturbing situations, and to seek or construct more simple and unified ones. It is a remarkable fact that most systems of philosophy seek to find some universal principle, law, ground, etc., which will explain the multiplicity of events. The tendency to explain things by simple reasons, and to connect phenomena through analogy is probably due to the same cause. Unity gives ease, rest, and satisfaction, and so is sought even when the seeking distorts truth.

The apparent discreteness in the field of visual attention in which from three to five objects seem to be discriminated at a single glance is due probably to retentiveness, development, and successive acts of attention upon memory images. Young children are not able to grasp as many objects at a single glance as are older children, and when the time of exposure of the objects is shortened, fewer are seen at once. When an individual sees four objects, he sees not four individual objects, but a group which is associated with 'fourness.' From long experience with such groups, *e.g.,* four corners, four fingers, etc., they come to mean 'four' to him. The association is one of words and meaning. Without such experience, as in the case of children, apprehension of objects becomes narrowed to one or two. When the objects are grouped they are seen as a 'four' group, a 'five' group, and the like. Practice will enable an individual to visualise groups containing a much larger number of objects. In the case of auditory fields, the rhythm probably takes the place of the visual group. The rhythm is apprehended as a whole, and by experience associated with 'four' or 'eight,' etc., as the case may be.

CHAPTER III
THE PSYCHOPHYSICAL ASPECT OF ATTENTION

§ I. DESCRIPTION

1. IDEAL. An impression in itself has little lasting power. It passes into consciousness and flits out without remaining long in the focus of attention. But little experience, however, is necessary to modify the pristine purity of impressions and to give them meaning one way or the other. Connections are made, ideal dispositions are formed, a mental set is developed, and what was originally a lone sensation is soon seized and held within the field of consciousness by the mental setting which has been acquired. Such ideal reinforcement may take the form of simple assimilation or of free association. Whichever be the case, the impression is lifted into the focus of consciousness and held there by ideal traces and dispositions.

(a) *Fusion, assimilation and complication.*[1]

[1] See Herbart, Johann Friedrich, *Sämmt. Werke,* herausgegeben von G. Hartenstein, 5:21-24, or *A Text-Book in Psychology,* Eng. tr. by M. K. Smith, Ch. III. Wundt, W., *Grund. d. Phys. Psych.,* Ch. XIX, § 2.

96

Each of these three forms of association deals with single moments of conscious apprehension. The incoming impression meets with ideal dispositions, and together these form a single perception, image, or idea. Fusion may be intensive, as in the case of sounds and feelings, or extensive, as in the case of visual and tactile impressions. In the former case a number of separate elements, as fundamental and overtones, are combined into a single complex called a tone. In the latter case visual elements as such, and motor elements are combined to give perceptions of distance, space and the like.

In assimilation, revived elements reinforce an impression, round it out, and give it meaning. A few strokes, for example, will outline the features of a known personage, while the beginning of a familiar word is usually all that is necessary to bring the whole to mind. The numerous proof reader's errors are an indication of such assimilation. Fluctuation of the more complex figures as the cube or the staircase may also be controlled in part by it.

Complication is a loose form of simultaneous association and may at times pass over into free association. Thus, attention to a piece of silk may excite the feel of it, and the sight of water

7

may revive the impression of wetness. A view
of a knife, too, may rouse tendencies to use it,
or the thought of some action may call up tendencies to motor control. Such associations may
be concomitant with the impression or idea. If
attention persists, such impressions or ideas may
unroll into a train of thought or a series of
reactions.

(b) *Free revival.* A situation may excite
an image, idea, or a series of ideas. Each in
turn will reinforce aspects of the situation in the
focus of attention and will keep it in the field
of clearness and distinctness. The field in the
focus of control may rouse images of previous
events connected with it, or of surroundings in
which it was experienced. It may revive an
ideal system to which it belongs, or ideas of other
situations to which it is a means, and which it
may help to realise. As idea after idea rises and
reinforces aspects of the situation under control, attention to the situation in question persists. The more ideal connections which can be
made, the longer will attention persist. Thus,
one may take a time-table and examine it for a
considerable time. The words and figures in
themselves can not hold the attention. But as
they are connected with persons, events, places,

memory images, and too often with the products of the imagination, they hold the centre of the attention field.

Considerable laboratory work has been done for the purpose of finding the forms of association which are possible in such ideal revival. It is found that a situation tends to revive an idea or an image of another situation with which it coexisted, or with which it is connected by some relation or series of relations. The former gives what is called synchronous association, or association by contiguity in time or place, the latter gives what is called association by similarity, cause and effect, purpose, design, or what not. Before giving a logical classification of situations which are represented by the revived images and ideas which act as reinforcing agents, it is necessary for one clearly to set forth what such a classification means. The terms 'contiguity,' 'similarity,' 'purpose,' etc., refer not to the ideas or images, but to the given situation, and the other situations with which it is or was connected in some way. Thus, if one attends to a book, and recalls bygone days when friends and companions were near by, the contiguity of such situations is in question, and not the contiguity of the ideas or images. So, too, if one recalls a book like the one attended to, the image refers to a similar book. The similarity is a relation existing between the objects and not between the ideas. The reason for such revival will be explained in a following section. Somewhat to anticipate, it may be noted that any contiguity or continuity of cerebral elements which underlies the ideal succession is very different from the contiguity of the situations when first experienced.

Keeping in mind that the classification which is given below refers to forms of association, and to relations which are possible between situations, one may have any of the following:

I. OF THINGS

1. QUANTITATIVE

(a) *Time*	(b) *Space*
Succession	Contiguity
Duration	Distance
Simultaneity	Direction

2. QUALITATIVE

Substance	and	Attribute
Whole	and	Part
Genus	and	Species

3. FORMAL

Causality	Contrast
Similarity	Purpose or Design

Signification or Meaning

II. OF PERSONS

1. SUPERIOR	2. EQUAL	3. SUBORDINATE
Ruler	Ruler-ruler	Subject
Employer	Subject-subject	Employee
Supervisor	Worker-worker	Worker
Parent	Parent-parent	Child
Etc.	Etc.	Etc.[2]

(c) *Deliberative.* When a situation excites a number of attitudes which prevent immediate control, the individual selects various aspects of the situation in question, thinks them over, refers to past experiences, to authority, etc., weighs evidence, and either decides one way or the other, or leaves the question unsettled. From the psychological point of view we say that there exists a conflict of ideas and motives, that there is present deliberation and choice. All the while that deliberation is going on, it is evident that the situation in question persists in the centre

[2] Some of the above classification has been suggested by Professor J. E. Lough, of New York University. See also Thorndike, E. L., 'Animal Intelligence,' *Psych. Rev., Mon. Sup.,* 4:65-109. For a number of other classifications see Trautscholdt, M., 'Experimentelle Untersuchungen über die Association der Vorstellungen,' *Phil. Stud.,* 1. Wundt, W., *Grund.,* 3:Ch. XIX. Cattell, J. McKeen, and Bryant, S., 'Mental Association Investigated by Experiment,' *Mind,* 14. Calkins, M. W., 'Association, An Essay Analytic and Experimental,' *Psych. Rev., Mon. Sup.,* 2. Claparède, E., *L'Association des Idées.* A summary of classifications will be found in Arnold, F., 'The Psychology of Association,' *Arch. of Phil., Psych. and Sci. Meth.,* 3.

of control. An individual who must pay the instalment on a mortgage and who is looking for means to collect the necessary money, is an example in point.

When conflict in deliberation is strong, and attention is more or less intense, feelings of strain arise. These feelings are felt especially about the head and eyes. With older psychologists this is sometimes mistaken as a sign of some general activity of attention or will which is supposed to stand over and above the process directing selection and choice. That such strain is due to peripheral stresses is shown by the following facts:

(1) Feeling of effort arises when there is conflict in deliberation, or when, in the process of attempted control, accommodation is inadequate, *i.e.,* when attention is not wholly effective. When attention is more effective, such feelings of strain tend to disappear. It is the problem which baffles, the situation which is troublesome, the flux of impossible conditions, etc., which cause worry and strain.

(2) If an individual strains his right arm in attempting to raise an object, he will feel a strain on the right side of his head. This would not be the case if the feeling of strain depended

upon psychophysical conditions. In such a case, they would be felt on the left side.[3]

(3) Increase in the intensity of attention is not always accompanied by more intense feelings of strain and effort. When one is beginning a task, or is attempting something new, or is taking up work long since forgotten, the preliminary adjustments excite more intense feelings of strain than later control. As control becomes more effective, and as attention increases in efficiency, feelings of effort tend to become less.

(4) One can produce the feeling of strain artificially. If one contracts the forehead intensely for a time, makes the scalp tense about the frontal region, and if possible draws the ears back, a feeling of strain will be noticed much like feelings of strain in mental deliberation. After concentrated mental work, the feeling of strain and incipient fatigue can be aggravated by these means. In all this, what is denied is not the existence of any psychophysical activity, but only its appearance, as such, in the realm of sensation. In referring to attention as selecting, discriminating, and the like, what one means is not some special activity, but the activity of the individual in attempting fuller control. His motor adjust-

[3] Münsterberg, H., *Die Willenshandlung*, 73.

ments and innervations, his ideas and images which reinforce incoming sensations, these, taken together, result in discrimination and produce clearness and distinctness.

2. CEREBRAL. In outlining the cerebral concomitants of mental activity, one must consider the ideal elements in connection with the motor. The functional unit is not sensory alone, but sensorimotor. In dealing with the psychological aspect, one may consider ideal and sensory elements apart from motor for purposes of discussion, but in treating the nervous substratum, the sensorimotor unit is best described by presenting it as it is, a connected whole.

(a) *Reflex*. The simplest sensorimotor arc is the reflex arc. A sensory stimulus is conducted by means of a sensory neuron to the posterior root of the spinal column, transferred to the anterior horn, and then is carried by means of one or more motor neurones to a muscle. This is the process which takes place at the level of the spinal column. The incoming stimulation proceeds by way of what are called afferent nerve fibres, the outgoing by way of efferent nerve fibres. Such an arc is made somewhat more complex by collateral fibres which branch out from the nerves and connect the different cells. The sensory fibres which enter the posterior roots may pass upwards and give off a number of collaterals, or they may connect with intermediate cells which in turn are connected with motor neurones. The process, however, is always a sensorimotor one.

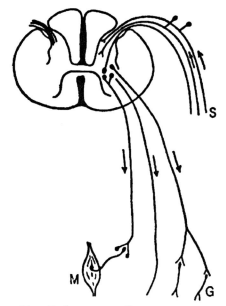

FIG. X.   Reflex arc.   S, sensory; M, motor.

Facilitation of motor reaction occurs when two or more sensory stimulations discharge into the same motor system. Inhibition or arrest occurs when two conflicting motor systems are simultaneously excited. The successful system in all probability then drains or diverts the energy excited by the stimulus which tended to excite the inhibited motor response. If, for example, *sa* and *sb,* two sensory stimuli, excite *ma* and *mb,* two motor nervous systems, *mb* may succeed in draining the energy excited in *ma* for its own use. This is a probable explanation of physiological inhibition or arrest.[4] Inhibition of spinal response may also be effected by cerebral activity. Paths already made by previous experiences in the cerebrum lead the energy generated by the stimulus into higher levels, and so change the nature of the response.

Skeletal arcs are connected with visceral arcs. The latter control respiration, heart-beat, dilation of arteries, etc. Reflex processes, besides terminating in an external motor response, may effect organic changes, as, changes in respiration, constriction of arteries, variation in heart-beat, and the like. Connections in the spinal cord between skeletal and visceral sensorimotor arcs are made by means of collateral fibres. In addition to connecting with motor nerve fibres, the sensory excitation may pass upwards and leave a trace in the cerebrum. The motor response may likewise be reflected back to a cerebral centre. Further connection is then made between the motor and sensory centres. It is this which gives a basis for higher, cerebral development.

[4] See McDougall, W., *Physiological Psychology,* 37.

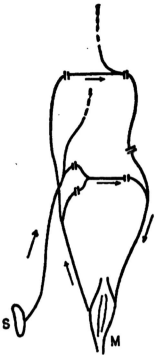

Fig. XI.   Sensimotor unit.
(After McDougal, *Mind*,
N. S., 12, 486.)

Sensorimotor arcs of the spinal level, in general, are characterised by (1) the relatively great constancy and regularity of their response to sensory stimuli, (2) their general vagueness and indistinctness in the field of consciousness, (3) their great freedom from interference or arrest by the activity of higher levels, and in many instances of their own level, and (4) their dependence upon sensory stimulation.[5]

(b) *Cerebral.* An important point to be noted

[5] See McDougall, W., 'The Physiological Factors of the Attention Process,' *Mind*, 11:341.

in the structure of higher cerebral levels is that the single cells are essentially of the same nature as those of the spinal level, that is, that they are sensorimotor.

Every part of the cortex receives incoming impulses and gives rise to outgoing impulses. Every part of the cortex is, therefore, both a termination of some afferent path and the beginning of some efferent path; it is, in other words, a reflex arc of a greater or less degree of complexity. We may suppose that every efferent discharge from any part of the cortex is occasioned by afferent impressions reaching that point from some other part of the nervous system. Whether or not there is such a thing as spontaneous mental activity cannot be determined by physiology, but on the anatomical side at least, all the structures exhibit connections that fit them for reflex stimulation, and many of our apparently spontaneous acts must be of this character.[6]

A second important feature in the structure of the cerebral level is the complexity and richness of the connections of the neurones.

This anatomical fact would indicate that the greater mental activity in the higher animals is dependent, in part, upon the richer interconnection of the nerve cells, or, expressed physiologically, our mental processes are characterised by their more numerous and complex associations. A visual or auditory stimulus that, in the frog

6 Howell, W. H., *Phys.*, 177.

for instance, may call forth a comparatively simple motor response, may in man, on account of the numerous associations with the memory records of the past experiences, lead to psychical and motor responses of a much more intricate and indirect character.[7]

In such a case, impressions start nervous impulses which instead of passing out immediately by way of the spinal cord, enter the cerebral loop and receive further direction there. The impulse proceeds then in the following order: (1) peripheral sense organ, (2) afferent nerve fibre, (3) spinal sensory cell, (4) afferent tract, (5) cortical sensory cell, (6) commissural fibre, (7) cortical motor cell, (8) efferent tract, (9) spinal motor cell, (10) efferent nerve fibre, and (11) muscle or peripheral end organ.[8]

The sensorimotor portion of the cerebrum consists of a number of more or less definitely localised centres. Among these are (1) the body sense area, (2) the visual centre, (3) the auditory centre, (4) the gustatory centre, (5) the speech centre, and (6) the motor area. Arcs of the cerebral level are characterised by (1) a less stable and fixed organisation, i.e., by a great variability in the direction of nervous discharge,

[7] *Ibid.*, 178-179.
[8] Waller, A. D., *An Int. to Hum. Phys.*, Ch. VIII.

(2) the increase in complexity and richness of interconnections, (3) the clearness and distinctness of the situations which correspond with their activity, (4) a general tendency of the activity of any system to inhibit the activity of any other system, and (5) their relative freedom from immediate sensory guidance.

(c) *Frontal.* Motor and sensory areas occupy the smaller portion of the cerebrum. The larger frontal region is occupied by what are now fairly well established as association areas.

The association areas may be regarded as the regions in which the different sense impressions are synthesised into complex perceptions or concepts. The foundations of all knowledge are to be found in the sensations aroused through the various sense organs; through these avenues alone can our consciousness come into relation with the external or the internal (somatic) world, and the union of these sense impressions is the general function of the association areas. This function of the association areas is indicated by the anatomical fact that they are connected with the various sense centres by tracts of association fibres. . . .

Here, as elsewhere in the nervous system, it may be supposed that the efficiency of the nervous machinery is conditioned partly by the completeness and character of training, but largely also by the inborn character of the machinery itself. The very marked differences among intelligent and cultivated persons—for instance, in the matter of musical memory and the power of appreciating and reproducing musical harmonies—cannot be attributed to differences of training alone. The gifted person in this respect is one who is born with a certain portion of his brain more highly organised than that of his fellow-men. . . . With our ideas of the organisation of the brain cortex, and our knowledge that different parts of this cortex give different reactions in consciousness, it seems to follow that special talents are due to differences in organisation of special parts of the cortex.[*]

§ II. ILLUSTRATION

1. IDEAL. (a) *Fusion, assimilation, complication.*

(1) *Literary.*

Under the pentacle I held the little boy, my workman. Now the necromancer began to utter those awful invocations, calling by name on multitudes of demons who are captains of their legions. . . . The boy, who was beneath the pentacle, shrieked out in terror that a million of the fiercest men were swarming round and threatened us. He said, moreover, that four huge giants had appeared, and were striving to force their way inside the circle.—I said to him: "These creatures are all inferior to us, and what you see is only smoke and shadow; so then raise your eyes."—*Memoirs of Benvenuto Cellini,* Book First, LXIV.

[*] Howell, W. H., *Phys.*, 210-211.

Errata in Villa, G., *Contemporary Psychology*, **xv.**

For Ralier *read* Rabier.

For Garofolo *read* Garofalo.

For Boratelli *read* Bonatelli.

For La coscienza nell' uomo *read* La coscienza nel sonno.

For Guiguo *read* Giugno.

For particular choice *read* particular chain.

For 1878 *read* 1898.

Explain these errors by assimilation, etc.   What was the sense core? What ideal elements were revived? What elements should have been revived?

(2) *Experimental.*

Find the concealed figures in the 'puzzle pictures.' How do they appear after they have once been found? Why do they appear so?[10]

Strike a chord on the piano.   Strike one of the single tones.   Strike the chord again and look for the single tone.   What is the result?   How does it sound relative to the others?

Why does the following illustration represent a soldier entering an inn with his dog?   What are the sensory elements?   What are the ideal factors?[11]

FIG. XII

[10] Titchener, E. B., *Exp. Psych.*, 1:Pt. I, 110.

[11] DeGarmo, Charles, *The Essentials of Method*, 25.

(3) Schematic.

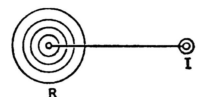

FIG. XIII.   I, impression.   R, revived disposition.

(b) Free association.

(1) Literary.

Wee, modest, crimson-tipped flow'r,
Thou's met me in an evil hour;
For I maun crush amang the stoure
  Thy slender stem:
To spare thee now is past my pow'r
  Thou bonnie gem.

Cauld blew the bitter-biting north
Upon thy early, humble birth;
Yet cheerfully thou glinted forth
  Amid the storm,
Scarce rear'd above the parent-earth
  Thy tender form.

Such fate to suffering Worth is giv'n,
Who long with wants and woes has striv'n,
By human pride or cunning driv'n
  To mis'ry's brink:
Till, wrench'd of ev'ry stay but Heav'n,
  He, ruin'd, sink!

    To a Mountain Daisy, Burns.

8

(2) Experimental.

Recall fully what you did with the book you read before this one. The centre of attention is 'book.'

Give three images, or ideas, or series of images or ideas which the following words recall: *light, money, boy, paper, country.*

Try to recall five ideas or images.

Classify your results according to the logical scheme in the preceding section. Remember that the words recalled represent objects or situations and it is the situations which are to be classified according to the scheme outlined.

Of the following, give the name of (1) a part, (2) an attribute, (3) a use, (4) an object like it, and (5) an object sometimes seen next to or near it: *book, knife, pen, dog, tree.*

How does this series of associations differ from the one above? What ideal reinforcement do these centres of attention receive?

What would you do if you received $5,000 on condition that you spend half of it in a reasonable manner within one day? The idea of the money is the centre of attention. What ideal elements keep it there?

(3) Schematic.

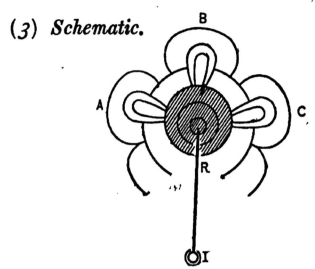

FIG. XIV. I, impression. R, revived disposition, A, B, C, etc., associations.

(c) Deliberative.

(1) Literary.

He's here in double trust;
First, as I am his kinsman and his subject,
Strong both against the deed; then, as his host,
Who should against his murderer shut the door,
Not bear the knife myself. Besides, this Duncan
Hath borne his faculties so meek, hath been
So clear in his great office, that his virtues
Will plead like angels trumpet-tongued against
The deep damnation of his taking-off;
And pity, like a naked new-born babe,
Striding the blast, or heaven's cherubim horsed
Upon the sightless couriers of the air,
Shall blow the horrid deed in every eye,
That tears shall drown the wind.

Macbeth, 1 :vii.

When he found I would leave him, he took care to prevent my getting employment in any other printing-house of the town, by going round and speaking to every master, who accordingly refus'd to give me work. I then thought of going to New York, as the nearest place where there was a printer; and I was rather inclin'd to leave Boston when I reflected that I had already made myself a little obnoxious to the governing party, and, from the arbitrary proceedings of the Assembly in my brother's case, it was likely I might, if I stay'd, soon to bring myself into scrapes; and farther, that my indiscrete disputations about religion began to make me pointed at with horror by good people as an infidel or atheist.—Franklin, *Autobiography*.

(*2*) *Experimental*.

Which is better, to work hard during youth, so that enjoyment and ease may come in later life, or to have a modicum of enjoyment and ease during youth, with the possibility of the same during old age?

If you come to any conclusion, give reasons for your conclusion. Upon what are they based? Is your reasoning more the result of personal attitude, or more the result of observation on the experience of others? Has your reading influenced your train of thought?

Why are you studying or reading psychology, or Greek, or English? What was your aim at first? What means other than study did you have in mind for reaching your aim? When you attended to the means, *i.e.*, when you were studying on a hot night or on a pleasant day, was the idea of the end always in view? Were there any conflicting ends, or situations?   When does the end rise to the focus of consciousness?   What effect has it on attention to the means?

(3) Schematic.

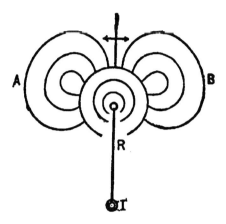

Fig. XV.   I, impression.   R, revived disposition.   A, B, conflicting associations.

2. CEREBRAL.

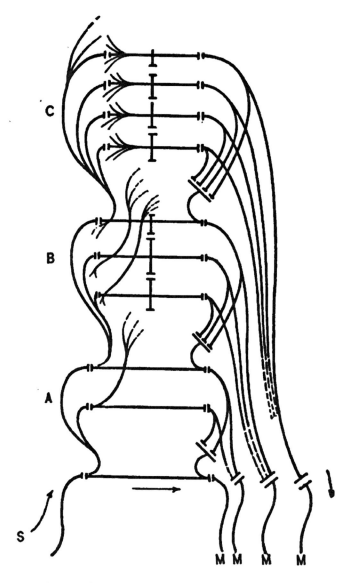

FIG. XVI.   S, sense impression.   M, motor response.
A, B, C, higher levels.   (After McDougall, W., *Mind*,
N. S., 11:888.)

§ III. DEVELOPMENT

1. IDEAL. The general order of development of the ideal dispositions which reinforce an impression or idea is from (1) impression to memory, (2) memory to ideal construction, and (8) ideal construction to deliberation and choice. The special direction given to such development is due in part to experience and training, in part to natural capacity and talent. Environment and heredity are two factors which condition specialisation and efficiency. The general order of progression, however, is as indicated above.

When an impression alone is able to control attention, we have primitive or instinctive attention. When attention in part is sustained by a series of ideas or images we have assimilative or apperceptive attention. When conflict, deliberation and choice are factors which keep a situation in the centre of attention, or when means are attended to because they are bound with an end, we have voluntary or selective attention. Other terms which are used are, passive and active, primary and secondary, involuntary and voluntary, etc. These aspects, be it noted, constitute only a part of the attentive process. The other and equally important part is the motor control.

(a) *Primitive or instinctive.* In its earliest

stages, attention is instinctive. A sudden noise, a differing or changing impression, or one pleasurable or painful, will stimulate reaction, will, in general, impel consciousness towards it. An infant, at times, seems to be controlled almost wholly by external impressions. Test any very young child, by moving the finger before it, or by tapping, or by holding a colored stick or ball within its grasp, and note the result.

(b) *Assimilative or apperceptive.* Such impressions leave traces which on the psychophysical side are called dispositions or memories. When some basis of experience has been constructed, impressions no longer pass through lower levels, but are guided and controlled in part by the activity of higher levels. Selection by means of ideal reinforcement is now possible. Of the multitude of impressions which flock in through the different sense organs, some persist in the centre of consciousness to the exclusion of other impressions. Some impressions have a meaning to the individual because of the experiences through which he has gone. Associations are excited, ideal dispositions are aroused, and these enable the impression, which is facilitated, to remain longer in the centre of greatest clearness and distinctness. A selection from an opera which has been sung at school, which has been heard from the street hand-organs, etc., stands out with special distinctness when heard at legitimate opera. From an individual point of view, conscious selection is in part nothing more than specialised ideal reinforcement of impressions which has been made possible through previous experience.

(c) *Secondary or voluntary.* In the course of experience, some situations yield pleasure, ease, satisfaction, quiescence, and a general attitude favorable towards their control. When such situations are not present, only traces remain in the form of memories, ideas, plans, and the like. Attempts to bring back such or similar situations, or to make them more stable, or to reconstruct them, impel attention both to the situation in question, and to means by which it may be realised. The situation is not present, or, if present, is not fixed. Possibilities of its realisation or fixation excite the idea of means which may bridge the gap between the future and the present. An attempt is made to direct present control and attention in such a way that thought and action will lead to what is desired. Deliberation and choice in such a case are due to the number of means which may be possible. Attention to the situation persists in part because of desires and anticipations of pleasure, in part to the series of ideas which arise out of the end to be sought. Such ideas are evolved out of the end to be realised, and out of the situation under immediate control. They serve to lead the individual from the present to that which is to be attained. A child, for example, who covets a toy, may plan to get it by saving his money, by coaxing his mother to get it, by making it himself, by exchanging something else for it, by taking it outright, and the like. In older persons, the means become more complicated. Sometimes years intervene between the beginning of attention to some means, and final realisation of the end.

The means which lead to the end may be attractive or repelling. In either case they are secondary and of themselves might not persist in the centre of attention. Attention to them persists because of the connections which they have with the situation which is to be realised. It is this characteristic which leads one to give to attention the name of voluntary, secondary, or acquired. Much of the work of the world is done because of such secondary attention. In fact, most of the stability and persistence of work is due to voluntary attention. No doubt much of the work may be able to hold attention for a time in itself, but irregularity and lapses are prevented because of the connection of such work with an end which is to be realised. An individual may, no doubt, like to sit behind his desk and do his work. But the flesh is weak, and at times, external stimulation, temptations, a pleasant day, alluring company, temporary indisposition, and the like would probably overcome the attractiveness of the work itself, were it not for the end to which the work leads, and which would fail of realisation if lapses crept in.

Schematically the process in attention may be represented somewhat as follows: A may represent an idea or image of the situation which is to be realised, as, a check, a pleasant time in the country, etc., and a, b, c, d, e, etc., the means which lead to A, as work, attention to a book, deprivation of temporary pleasures, and the like. If the desire for A is strong enough, attention to a, b, c, etc., will persist because of their association with A. The means, a, b, c, etc., may or may not be pleasurable. They may hold attention simply because they lead to a satisfying or pleasurable situation. Should they develop associations of their own they might then hold attention in themselves. Such attention would then be assimilative or apperceptive as above described. One who reads history or psychology at first for the purpose of passing an examination, may in time come to like it for its own sake.

Deliberation is usually necessary when two conflicting ends strive to hold the focus of consciousness, or when the proper means are to be selected for the solution of a problem, or for effective guidance to the end in view. In such a process ideal series are referred back to the situation in question, tested, applied, connected with further associations, referred again to the situation in the focus of attention, etc., and then finally accepted or rejected. The individual who desires to go to the country may inquire, visit different places, seek means of travel, arrange money matters, check himself here or there to ensure effective control, and so on. The process is one with which most are familiar.

On the ideal side the general order of development is somewhat as follows:

(1) Instinctive reaction to difference, change, or pleasure-pain.

(2) Attention reinforced by some form of association.

(3) Attention to agreeable means which lead to some situation not far distant.

(4) Attention to agreeable means which lead to some situation far distant.

(5) Attention to disagreeable means which lead to a situation soon to be realised.

In the above discussion, only the ideal elements have been presented. It must be remembered, however, that the entire process is a sensorimotor one, and that ideal reinforcement is only a part of the process.

2. CEREBRAL. In cerebral development, the first centres to be developed are those of smell, sight, hearing, touch, and body sense (skin and muscles). Soon after this, the motor fibres appear. These are called the primary zone areas and have projection fibres, both sensory and motor. Later still, the association areas acquire their myelinated or sheathed fibres. Upon anatomical grounds the order of development may be said to be from sensorimotor impression to association and differentiation.[12]

(a) *Reflex*. The simplest act of attention from the cerebral side is an instinctive response to an external impression. A light, a sound, a sudden touch, etc., impel the sense organs to instinctive adjustment. Further response may also be excited. The nervous impulse passes

[12] Howell, W. H., *Phys.*, Ch. X.

by way of the spinal cord to some motor neuron. In addition, it passes up and leaves a trace in a sense tract of the cerebrum. The motor impulse, after effecting muscular response, produces a muscular sensation. This likewise is carried back to the brain and deposited in the corresponding sense tract. By these means experience leaves its mark on the individual, and builds up a sensorimotor basis for further use.

(b) *Cerebral.* The various traces which are left in the cortex are connected in different degrees of complexity. Visual combine with auditory and tactile impressions, and all lead in some way to the motor areas. Upon later excitation they serve to reinforce impulses which come from without. According as experience has developed traces will some cerebral dispositions be roused and others not. In other words, some impressions are selected or discriminated by the individual, and others inhibited. A botanist will see a flower in a light different from that of a florist. A cook may see in it something different from that which attracts the attention of either. In cerebral terms, discrimination and selection mean simply nervous reinforcement of an impression by means of residual traces of former experiences. No doubt natural tendencies have something to do with the acquiring of such experiences. But any cerebral reinforcement is dependent upon traces left by former impressions and reactions.

(c) *Frontal.* On the cerebral side further development consists in the connections which are made among the various traces left. Since many association fibres acquire their sheaths only late in life, and some not at all, it is evident that increase in the complexity of associations proceeds so long as the individual is active. Development in this connection is by no means restricted to the years of childhood. In voluntary attention, considerable motor control is necessary. On the cerebral side, however, there is nothing to indicate that in such attention the cerebral process is anything more than association and predominance of some system of dispositions.

In cases of voluntary reactions the impulses take a longer pathway and involve a larger series of central nerve-elements, since from the point at which they enter the system they must pass to the cephalic end and back again to the efferent elements. At the same time, in a voluntary action, a greater number of impulses combine to modify the discharge from the efferent cells.[18]

Any feeling of strain which may be felt in

[18] *American Text-Book of Physiology,* 2:226.

voluntary attention is simply sensation of muscular effort, end-organ adjustments, etc., as pointed out in a preceding section.

§ IV. EXPLANATION

1. IDEAL. When an impression is lifted into the centre of attention, clothed with meaning, and reinforced by associations, one underlying law can be found to explain the process. The present moment on the ideal side consists of the impression, p, plus the revived elements which give to p its meaning and direction. The total state may be represented by pmn, in which m represents the meaning due to ideal revival, and n the tendency to pass onwards in the direction developed by previous experience. This whole moment then may excite a series of ideas or images which in themselves have meanings and tendencies. The process of revival may be represented by the series,

$$p\,m_x\,n_y,\ a\,m_1\,n_1\ b\,m_2\,n_2\ c\,m_3\,n_3\ \cdot\ \cdot\ \cdot\ etc.$$

These moments represent the process on the ideal side. If we represent the objects which correspond or have at some time corresponded with the mental states we have,

$$p\,m_x\,n_y,\ a\,m_1\,n_1\ b\,m_2\,n_2\ c\,m_3\,n_3\ \cdot\ \cdot\ \cdot\ etc.\ \textit{Mental}$$
$$1\,1^1\,1^2\ \ 2\,2^1\,2^2\ \ 3\,3^1\,3^2\ \ 4\,4^1\,4^2\ \cdot\ \cdot\ \cdot\ etc.\ \textbf{\textit{Physical}}$$

For example, suppose I attend to the book before me. This is a definite object, and corresponds to $1, 1^1$, etc., according as I have seen it a number of times in various connections. If I continue to look at it I may recall the store in which I bought it, the persons whom I met at the time, the use to which I have put it, and so on. Such ideas are represented by am_1n_1, bm_2n_2, etc. But the actual situation, the store, for example, is represented by $2, 2^1$, etc. If we consider the mental states we can formulate some one law which will explain the ideal succession. If we consider the objects, however, to which the mental states correspond, as book-store, etc., we have forms or relations of association which give us contiguity, similarity, purpose, or what not. These points of view, if confused, lead to a misconception of the law of psychophysical association.[14]

The law which underlies the ideal revival of reinforcing dispositions may be stated as follows:

Any element tends to reinstate the entire moment of which it constitutes a part, which moment tends (1) to diffuse itself along some one of the paths

[14] See Arnold, F., 'The Unity of Mental Life,' *Jour. Phil., Psych., and Sci. Meth.,* 2. 'Association and Atomism,' *ibid.* 'The Initial Tendency in Ideal Revival,' *Am. Jour. of Psych.,* 18.

9

which have been formed, and (2) to leave
a trace of itself as a whole for future revival
and development.

What we have is neither contiguity nor similarity, but rather continuity of ideal processes.
Contiguity, similarity, etc., refer to the objects
correspondent with the ideas.

The special direction which such diffusion will
take depends upon various factors in previous
experience. These give rise to what are called
extrinsic secondary laws of association, namely,
(1) repetition, (2) vividness, (3) recency, (4)
primacy, and (5) emotional congruity. They
may be stated briefly as follows:

(1) Situations which are frequently presented
tend to develop dispositions which are readily
revived.

(2) Situations which are vivid tend to leave
traces which are readily revived.

(3) Situations which have been recently experienced tend to leave traces which are readily
revived.

(4) First impressions tend to leave traces
which are readily revived.

(5) Situations which excite an emotion leave
traces which are readily revived when the emotional attitude is again taken even if for differ-

ent reasons. Revivability may be caused by reappearance of the situation itself, or, according to the law of association just given, by any other situation which has common elements, or which is objectively or formally connected with it as suggested in the forms or relations of association outlined in a section above. Thus, similar memories may be roused by the sight of a friend, of his photograph, of his name, of a present from him, etc. The stimulus serves to rouse the whole disposition, which then diffuses in different directions.

The secondary laws are probably variations of the one law of repetition. Thus, a vivid situation will leave a trace which is readily revived upon another occasion. This gives repetition of the revival with further associations. Such associations may stimulate other revivals, with increased repetition. So the process continues. First impressions operate in a similar manner. Thus, early impressions in childhood are constantly resurrected by our home surroundings, friends, household gods, and the like. So, by repetition, they become imbedded more deeply in the memory. The same holds true to a certain extent for emotional congruity, and for recency. At bottom, repetition of impressions and revivals is the most important means by which direction, order, and organization of associations become fixed.

On the subjective side we have as intrinsic secondary laws of association, (1) organisation, (2) comprehensiveness, (3) coöperation and strength of cohesiveness between parts, (4) the nature of the predominating sensory elements, and (5) general conditions of freshness and vitality of the individual.[15] Such organisation and systemisation will depend in part upon natural tendencies, and in part upon environment and education. Briefly stated these intrinsic secondary laws are:

(1) The direction and the duration of ideal diffusion and association are dependent upon the organisation of the mental dispositions aroused.

(2) The number of associations which can be revived depends upon the comprehensiveness of the ideal systems excited.

(3) The persistence of any ideal system depends upon the strength and number of its various parts.

(4) The quality or the ideas or images revived depends upon the predominating sensory elements.

(5) Organisation, comprehensiveness, etc., are

[15] Stout, G. F., *Analytic Psychology*, 2:Ch. VII, § 6-8.

more or less effective in facilitating the ease and duration of revival according as the individual is rested or fatigued.

The function of the ideas, images, and dispositions which are revived are (1) to reinforce incoming impressions and to inhibit others, *i.e.,* to discriminate and select, and (2) to give guidance to motor attitudes and control. The former has already been described. A word or two is necessary to emphasise the latter. Ideas and images in themselves are bleak and barren. Only as they are accompanied by attitudes or more open motor response do they have life and reality. Even the most abstruse and speculative inquiries give forth tendencies and lead to attitudes which ·are satisfying, pleasurable, or the reverse. Such attitudes stand for, and in a way, represent the fuller motor explication which would follow in complete realisation of the ideas. This motor attitude will be considered fully in the next chapter.

2. CEREBRAL. A sensory stimulus leads to a motor discharge because the nervous paths are organised that way. All nervous impulses pass in a forward direction from sense organ to sensory cells, and then to motor cells and to the muscles. In reflex and instinctive responses the

sensory stimulation alone is sufficient to open the nerve paths and start the complete sensori-motor process.

In acquired responses, paths between the cortical cells are probably broken through by the localised emphasis of the tonic activity of the nervous system. The more or less uniform nervous pressure which is present during the waking state is raised in intensity by sensory stimulation. A heightened activity is thus produced in some of the cortical cells. Such activity flows forward towards motor cells. It also drains cells connected with those excited by sensory stimulation. When several sensory cells are excited, the heightened diffusion of nervous energy in restricted portions of the cortex probably opens up connecting paths between them, some by pressure, some by drainage.[16] Later excitations will then flow in such paths as have been opened, *i.e.,* will pass along the line of least resistance. Individual capacity and organisation of cerebral cells and fibres may likewise condition the kinds of connections which can be made.

The nervous processes which go on in acts of attention may be briefly explained. When a sensory impression is reinforced by an ideal dis-

[16] James, W., *Princ. of Psych.,* 2:580-592.

position or a series of dispositions, the correspondent cerebral process is somewhat as follows:
The nervous impulse passes along lines of least
resistance to the cortex and diffuses into channels which have been formed by previous experience.   Tonic activity of the cerebrum becomes
heightened and focalised within narrow sensorimotor limits.   Motor responses may result in
further discrimination and selection of aspects
of the situation and so give rise to more impressions, and stimulate greater sensorimotor activity.
In abstract thought motor attitudes may serve
the same purpose.   The question of motor response is, in fact, one of the most important in
the attentive process.[17]

[17] Baldwin, J. Mark, *Mental Development in the Child and the
Race*, Ch. XIV.

CHAPTER IV
THE PHYSIOLOGICAL ASPECT OF ATTENTION

§ I. DESCRIPTION

1. ORGANIC. Attention to a situation is marked by a number of organic changes, some of which are more or less constant. The general organic changes involve (1) respiration, (2) vasomotor constriction of peripheral arteries, and (3) circulation.[1]

[1] Among others see Angell, James Rowland, and Thompson, Helen Bradford, 'A Study of the Relations between Certain Organic Processes and Consciousness,' *Psych. Rev.*, 6:32-69. MacDougall, Robert, 'The Physical Characteristics of Attention,' *Ibid.*, 3:158-180. McGamble, Eleanor A., 'Attention and Thoracic Breathing,' *Am. Jour. of Psych.*, 16:261-292. Mentz, Paul, 'Die Wirkung akustischer Sinnesreize auf Puls und Athmung,' *Phil. Stud.*, 11:61-124, 371-393, 563-602. Zoneff, P., und Meumann, E., 'Ueber Begleiterscheinungen psychischer Vorgänge in Athem und Puls,' *Phil. Stud.*, 18:1-113. Stevens, H. C., 'A Plethysmograph Study of Attention,' *Am. Jour. of Psych.*, 16:409-483. J. J. van Biervliet, 'Ueber den Einfluss der Geschwindigkeit des Pulses auf die Zeitdauer der Reactionszeit by Schalleindrücken,' *Phil. Stud.*, 10:160-167, and 'Ueber den Einfluss der Geschwindigkeit des Pulses auf die Zeitdauer der Reactionszeit bei Licht- und Tasteindrücken,' *Ibid.*, 11:125-134. Delabarre, Edmond B., 'L'Influence de L'Attention sur les Mouvements Respiratoires,' *Rev. Phil.*, 33:639-649. Bonser, F. G., 'A Study of the Relations between Mental Activity and the Circulation of the Blood,' *Psych. Rev.*, 10:120-138. Binet, A. and Vaschide, N., 'The Influence of Intellectual Work on the Blood-Pressure in Man,' *Ibid.*, 4:54-66.

(a) *Respiration.* Concentrated attention usually gives rise to rapid, shallow breathing. The inspiration becomes shorter, the expiration shorter, and the rate more rapid. The respiration may be slightly inhibited. Variations are possible, both in the rate and depth of the respirations.

(b) *Vasoconstriction.* When the volume of the hand or finger is measured during attention, it usually shows a decrease due to a sympathetic constriction of the peripheral arteries. Such constriction may be slowly succeeded by a gradual dilation of the arteries to the normal. It may be accompanied by dilation of the cerebral arteries and increase in the supply of blood to the brain.

(c) *Circulation.* During attention the pulse becomes more rapid. There is always some variation in the pulse during concentrated attention of any kind. There is also found a change in blood pressure due in part to change in heart beat and in part to vasoconstriction of the arteries. Blood pressure tends to increase during periods of attentive activity. There seems likewise to be a redistribution of the supply which favors those areas which have been called into service. In moments of concentrated mental application it seems that the brain receives a greater supply of blood. It also shows a rise in temperature.

2. SENSORY. On the side of sensory accommodation and fixation attention consists of (1) changes within the organ itself which facilitate adjustment, and (2) motor adaptations for the purpose of fixation.

(a) *Accommodation*. In vision, the following changes take place during visual attention:

(1) There is adaptation of the pupil which controls the admission of light and so conditions visual distinctness and clearness.

(2) The surface of the lens changes, becoming more convex in the middle and flatter towards the periphery.[2]

When external conditions are artificially varied the following changes may be noted:

(1) When the eyes fixate a spot directly ahead and at the same time attend to an object out of line with direct vision, the pupil shows an increase in size.

(2) When the light is decreased in intensity the pupil increases in size.

(3) In mental processes which require no im-

[2] Tscherning, M., *Physiological Optics*, Eng. tr. by C. Weiland, Ch. XII.

mediate use of vision the pupil expands the most. At the same time the lens becomes correspondingly flatter.[3]

Changes in the other sense organs are not so evident. In audition it is highly probable that the two intrinsic muscles of the ear, the tensor tympani and the stapedius, function as a means of accommodation for the tympanic membrane and for the membrane attached to the base of the stapedius. In tasting, the increased flow of saliva, and in smelling, the increased dilation of the nostrils and the stronger inhalations likewise function to bring about distinctness and clearness in the field of attention.

(b) *Fixation.* Control of a sensory situation involves fixation of the end organs. If the situation is a visual one, the eyes turn towards it and focus it. If auditory, the head turns in the direction of the sound. If tactile, the fingers feel and touch it. If gustatory, the tongue rolls it about and takes different shapes and positions. The whole mechanism seeks to produce clearness and distinctness. Accurate observations have been made in visual fixation. The movements of the eye have been photographed

[3] Heinrich, W., 'Die Aufmerksamkeit und die Funktion der Sinnesorgane,' *Zeit. f. Psych. u. Phys. d. Sinnesorg.,* 9:342-388

both in general fixation and in reading. It is
shown by such photographs that the eye, in fixating a point, does not remain rigid, but fixates
around the point, covering a small area. Moreover, the two eyes are not exactly, but only approximately coördinate in fixating a point or in
passing over a line from one end to the other.[4]
In reading, the eyes cover the printed page by a
series of rapid movements from left to right.
These movements vary in number between 2 and
7 for a single line and usually number from 4 to
6. A slight pause occurs between each movement
and the one which follows it. The area which can
be seen at any single moment is represented ap-

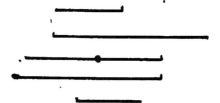

FIG. XVII. Visual field in reading (After Huey, E. B., *Psych.
and Ped. of Read.*, 52).

proximately by the following diagram. By fixating the central dot one can see the letters

[4] *Yale Psychological Studies, Psych. Rev., Mon. Sup.,* 7, 'Intro-
duction to a Series of Studies of Eye Movements by Means of
Kinetoscopic Photographs,' C. H. Judd, C. N. McAllister, and
W. M. Steele, 'The Fixation of Points in the Visual Field,' C. N.
McAllister.

written within the given area. It seems that 'more is read to the right of the fixation point than to the left.'[5]

(3) MOTOR. An important factor in the attention process is the motor aspect. Even when actual motor control is not in operation, motor attitudes and innervations serve instead to give meaning to a situation and to effect satisfaction, ease, quiescence, or pleasure. The motor aspect of attention usually assumes three forms, (1) motor diffusions, (2) motor innervations or attitudes, and (3) complete motor control.

(a) *Motor diffusion*. That ideas and images tend to realise themselves in action may be seen in moments of intellectual application. Hand, head and body movements indicate that nervous impulses are passing through motor channels. The head, face, fingers, and feet seem to be affected the most. A careful study of such automatic movements has been made by Lindley and the results of his findings are given below.[6] The

[5] Huey, Edmund Burke, *The Psychology and Pedagogy of Reading*, Ch. III. See also Dearborn, W. F., 'The Psychology of Reading,' *Arch. of Phil., Psych., and Sci. Meth.*, 4.

[6] Lindley, Ernest H., 'A Preliminary Study of Some of the Motor Phenomena of Mental Effort,' *Am. Jour. of Psych.*, 8:491-517.

general grouping of such movements is seen in the following:

Head: Held on side, move sideways, move up and down, move with pen, jerky movements, move.

Face: Grin, grimace.

Eyes: Fixed, wink, close, twitch, roll, squint, bulge.

Ears: Move.

Forehead: Wrinkle, frown.

Mouth: Twitch, drop corners, chew, move.

Jaw: Bite, chew, put objects in, clench, move sideways.

Lips: Draw in and out, pucker, move, work, bite, press, twist, suck, chew.

Tongue: Protrude, move sideways, move in and out, move with pen, bite, chew, roll in one cheek, suck.

Hands: Play, clasp, clench, rub or scratch, put in pocket, wriggle, pull hairs, etc., twist hair, smooth, put objects in, move.

Fingers: Play, drum, mark on paper, move up and down, point, move, snap, pull.

Arms: Fold and unfold, jerky movements.

Legs: Cross, move, move knees, twist, raise heel, twist heel.

Feet: Sides of feet, stand on one foot, right on left, left on right, rise on toes, rock, lift one foot, move, stamp, wriggle, cross, tap, shake.[7]

In addition, the following tables give the automatisms most frequent with children and adoles-

[7] *Ibid.,* 493.

cents, and also the movements characteristic of various activities:

	I Ch.	II Ad.	III Ch. 1.81	IV A	Freq. Ch.	Freq. Ad.	A'
Fingers	81	143	146	109	Fingers	Fingers	Head+
Feet	72	57	130.3	228	Feet	Feet	Mouth+
Lips	71	53	128	241	Lips	Eyes	Legs+
Tongue	57	26	103	396	Tongue	Lips	Tongue+
Head	48	8	86.8	1085	Head	Hands	Face+
Body	42	33	76	230	Body	Jaw	Lips+
Hands	32	49	57.9	118	Hands	Forehead	Body+
Mouth	20	6	36.2	603	Mouth	Body	Feet+
Eyes	15	56	27	48	Eyes	Tongue	Hands+
Jaw	13	49	23.5	47	Jaw	Head	Fingers+
Legs	6	2	10.8	540	Legs	Mouth	Arms—
Forehead	5	34	9.05	26	Forehead	Legs	Eyes—
Face	3	2	5.43	271	Face	Face	Jaw—
Arms	1	2	1.81	90	Arms	Arms	Forehead—
Ears		2			Ears	Ears	Ears—

I Ch.=children.

II Ad.=adolescents.

III Ch.=no. ch. x 1.81, there being 1.81 more adolescents than children reported.

IV A=percentages of children's automatisms as compared with adolescents.

A'=percentages arranged in order, + meaning more and — less for children.

TABLE XXXVII

The following is a classification according to activity:

WRITING	READING	RECITING	PUB. RECIT.	CONVERSATION	ATTENT. INT.	STUDYING	DIFFICULT REC.	GREATEST EFFORT
Lips 240	Body 240	Feet 253	Fingers	Fingers 433	Feet 421	Fingers 196	Eyes 339	Lips 258
Tongue 220	Head 180	Fingers 190	Body	Hands 170	Fingers 131	Hands 175	Hands 190	Hands 195
Head 170	Hands 140	Body 166	Eyes	Forehead 170	Hands 105	Jaw 163	Lips 127	Forehead 173
Feet 170	Fingers 140	Eyes 130	Hands	Legs 113	Lips 105	Lips 103	Body 84	Eyes 86
Mouth 87	Feet 110	Hands 120	Feet	Eyes 56	Eyes 78	Eyes 93	Head 73	Jaw 65
Forehead 24	Lips 55	Jaws 47	Head	Jaw 18	Forehead 78	Feet 92	Forehead 67	Fingers 65
Body 24	Tongue 36	Forehead 23	Jaw	Body 18	Jaw 52	Tongue 91	Fingers 64	Feet 43
Legs 24	Arms 18	Lips 23	Lips	Head 18	Legs 26	Body 21	Feet 63	Tongue 43
Jaw 14	Jaw 18	Head 15			Body	Forehead 21	Jaw 60	
Fingers 4		Face 15			Head	Legs 10	Face 30	
Hand 4		Arms 15			Ears	Face 10	Mouth 12	
						Head	Tongue 8	
						Arms		
						Ears		
No. cases 96	28	109	44	28	47	170	29	30
Av. per 100 214	180	110	120	100	186	130	160	160

TABLE XXXVIII

The direction of the motor diffusions may be determined by the following test: A plate glass, made opaque, rests on three ball bearings. Attached to the frame around the glass is a rod. At the end of the rod is a cork. Through the cork is a pencil. Under the pencil is a smoked paper. When the hand is placed on the plate glass and attention is concentrated on something else, the direction of the movements as recorded on the smoked paper will indicate roughly the direction of the attention. Jastrow found that the hand moves in the direction of colors when they are recognised and named in horizontal rows, and from left to right or the reverse when they are named from left to right or from right to left. So, too, the hand movement tends to accompany the rhythm in counting the beats of a metronome, or, if not, to move towards the sound. In thinking of some hidden objects, the marks on the paper indicate roughly the direction in which the objects lie.[3]

(*b*) *Motor innervation.* The tests just mentioned may be considered in part as evidence of motor innervation. Definite tests by Münsterberg and Campbell point to the same thing. If

[3] Jastrow, Joseph, 'A Study of Involuntary Movements,' *Am. Jour. of Psych.*, 4:398–407.

10

an observer gazes at an object, closes his eyes, and then turns his head sideways, the eyes lag somewhat behind the head rotation, and in fact may not turn at all. This is shown by measuring the head rotation in degrees and the correspondent eye rotation, also in degrees. The subject opens his eyes as soon as he has finished turning his head, and the rotation of the eyes is immediately measured. The following diagram shows a phase of the relative positions of head and eyes:

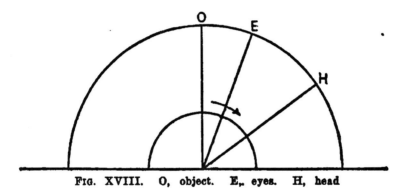

FIG. XVIII.   O, object.   E, eyes.   H, head

Even though the head has turned from *O* to *H,* the eyes still tend to fixate *O* which was looked at before the turning of the head began. The following tables show the difference between the head and the eye rotations, such differences being conditioned by the nature of the stimulating object:[9]

[9] Münsterberg, H., and Campbell, W. C., 'The Motor Power of Ideas,' *Psych. Rev.,* 1:441-453.

OBSERVER M

	1 second		2 second		3 second		4 second		Average	
	E	H	E	H	E	H	E	H	E	H
Letters	12	50	25	48	48	52	48	50	33	50
One word	13	46	25	46	47	47	47	52	33	48
Nine words	0	48	8	49	17	48	28	50	13	49
Picture	14	46	32	50	45	52	47	47	35	49
Nine pictures	0	45	0	47	2	50	16	49	5	48
One color	4	48	28	47	31	50	47	52	28	49
Two colors	4	47	22	47	23	46	46	48	24	47 ·
Irregular colors	0	46	16	48	25	50	39	51	20	49
Photo- graph	5	52	15	51	22	52	28	50	18	51
Num. for addition	42	52	47	47	42	52	44	49	44	50
Average	9.4	48.0	21.8	48.0	30.2	49.9	39.0	49.8	25.1	48.9

OBSERVER S

	1 second		2 second		3 second		4 second		Average	
Average	17.4	36.0	14.8	36.6	17.9	36.0	17.9	35.7	17.0	36.1

OBSERVER C

	1 second		2 second		3 second		4 second		Average	
Average	26.7	41.6	21.6	43.0	20.4	42.4	19.3	42.8	22.25	54.25

TABLE XXXIX

All three subjects agree that a simple letter, word, color, or picture has the weakest motor influence; all agree that two colors have more power than one, and the irregular colors still more . . . ; that nine pictures have by far stronger motor energy than one . . . ; nine

words stronger than one . . . ; that the photograph of
a person has far stronger motor function than the simply
sketched picture of an object of daily life.[10]

Images and ideas are strongly reinforced by
motor innervations, especially when conflict arises
or when greater distinctness is desired. In tests
on the fluctuation of visual fields or changing
perspectives, eye movements will reinforce one
aspect at the expense of the other. Thus, if one
fixates the staircase figure or the cube figure,
motor innervations will determine in part whether
the figure is to jut forward or retreat backward.
In fixating a field of white dots on a black background, the form, as, square, circle, triangle, etc.,
into which the spots fall, may be determined in
part by innervations of the eye muscles and the
head.

Memory images of objects and places are
made more definite by such innervations and
movements. Distinctness and clearness are facilitated by these motor aids, especially when
shape, or size, or position, are in doubt. Situations of greater complexity, as those which involve mechanical arrangements, movements of
parts, machinery, and the like, can often be
attended to only by the aid of motor tendencies

[10] *Ibid.,* 451-452.

felt in the fingers, hands, body, and head. At times, such tendencies become realised in actual movements, or in the definite construction of schematic diagrams. Only by such aids can the ideal situation persist in the centre of attention.[11]

In more abstract application, the motor attitudes are usually overlooked. There will be found, however, pauses and intermissions in which the series of ideas or images is followed by a more or less definite motor attitude, or even by motor reactions. There may be a shake of the head, a body tendency towards or from some ideal situation, hand and finger movements to emphasise affirmation and negation, in short, a general attitude which determines in what direction further thought should go. In addition to such definite pauses, there is a constant interplay between ideas and innervations, in which the former are tested, as it were, in a tentative manner. These motor innervations give rise to a feeling tone and reinforce one or the other series of ideas. In such cases the motor innervations and attitudes stand for actual manipulation and control. They give approximately similar feel-

[11] See Lange, N., 'Beiträge zur Theorie der sinnlichen Aufmerksamkeit und der activen Apperception,' *Phil. Stud.*, 4:413–422. Stricker, S., *Studien über die Sprachvorstellungen.* Münsterberg, H., *Beiträge zur Experimentellen Psychologie*, Heft 2.

ings of satisfaction, pleasure, and the like. If the attitude is not sufficient to determine the validity of some train of thought, then actual motor control often follows. This process will be found even in the most abstruse and speculative inquiries.[12]

(c) *Motor control.* Actual manipulation is most in evidence (1) when the child is first learning objective values, (2) when attention involves full control, and (3) when the meaning of an image or idea can not be determined or directed by motor innervations and attitudes, *i.e.,* when there is conflict of meaning or doubt. When a new situation is presented to an individual or when he is suddenly confronted with it, attention, on the motor side, is characterised by an excess of movements. If satisfactory control is not immediately realised, a number of manipulations, some effective, some ineffective, are attempted. Out of a large number of movements, some are capped with pleasure, satisfaction, etc., and tend to persist. So long as control yields pleasure or satisfaction, the situation will tend to persist in consciousness.[13]

[12] See Messer, August, 'Experimentell-psychologische Untersuchungen über das Denken,' *Arch. f. d. ges. Psych.,* 8: 1-224, § 8

[13] Baldwin, J. M., *Ment. Dev.,* Ch. VII.

Attention to objective situations consists largely of manual and similar adjustments. The object may be felt in a passive way, all parts of the hand coming into contact with it at once (synthetic touch), or the hand may explore the objective actively point by point (analytic touch).[14]   Dissection, application, and reconstruction may change the situation entirely, affording new bases for sensory stimulation and yielding a richer meaning to the individual. The persistence of the attention will depend largely upon the points of contact which are possible by such motor control and upon the stimulations which can be produced by manual manipulation and reconstruction. A child, for example, who has a few blocks, will obtain a certain amount of visual stimulation from them. If he builds with them and rearranges them, he will give rise to a new source of stimulation. As he continues to play with them his different reconstructions enable his attention to persist because of the varying situations which are afforded.[15]

In the last analysis, validity of judgment can be established only by application through motor

---

[14] Stout, G. F., *A Manual of Psychology*, Ch. IV.

[15] See MacDougall, Robert, 'The Significance of the Human Hand in the Evolution of Mind,' *Am. Jour. of Psych.*, 16:232-242.

means. An idea is tested by being applied to concrete situations. Where a motor basis has been established by experience, an attitude may take the place of more explicit realisation. In all such cases attention consists in the alternating process of ideal reinforcements and motor inner-vations. In both motor and ideal control, empha-sis upon any aspect of a situation necessarily excludes other aspects. There is no special and separate activity of inhibition in such a case. Inhibition is simply a name for the negative aspect of reinforcement. Aspects of a situation which are not effective in exciting ideal dispo-sitions or which are foreign to motor control will be unable to persist in the focus of attention, other things remaining the same. Such lack of persistence is called inhibition. Inhibition usu-ally implies predominance of some other aspect of a situation.[16] Such inhibition becomes more and more prominent as the grooves of habit and thought become deeper. It corresponds with that which from the social point of view is called conservatism. As individuals grow older, new situations have less and less chance to excite attention or to persist in the focus of control.

[16] See the excellent discussion in Mill, James, *Analysis of the Phenomena of the Human Mind,* Ch. XXIV.

The periods when impressions are able by virtue of their own inherent impelling power to excite attention are the plastic ages of childhood and youth.

4. FATIGUE. Concentrated activity, especially when it involves motor control, usually results in fatigue. There arises decreased irritability and increased slowness of response. Efficiency of attention begins to decline. In attention to minimal stimuli, the fluctuation periods become shorter. In simple reactions, the reaction time becomes longer. Objects in the field of attention persist for a less time in the centre of control. On the subjective side, fatigue is felt as weariness, disinclination to persistent effort, sensation of strain in the muscles, lack of interest in situations which normally are of an impelling nature, and sometimes as pain in the parts of the body affected. On the objective side, fatigue is manifested by a general slackness and listlessness of the body posture, by relaxed fingers, and by asymetrical and fidgety movements. Coördinations become more bungling, incorrect, and for finer control, often impossible. The eyes wander, lose the power of persistent fixation, and assume a general vacant expression. Response to stimulation becomes less exact and

requires more time than usual.   In more advanced stages of fatigue, there is a loss of control, a great irritability, and an explosiveness which may be set off by trifling stimulation.[17] General bodily fatigue results in a general depletion of nervous energy and by diffusion affects all portions of the organism.   Fatigue, however, may be localised in one or other sphere of activity.   In such a case continued activity within the sphere will give rise to manifestations of fatigue much like those of general fatigue.

§ II. ILLUSTRATION

1. ORGANIC.

(a) Literary.

Naturally enough the idea occurred to me: if the indentations on paper could be made to give forth again the click of the instrument, why could not the vibrations of a diaphram be recorded and similarly reproduced?   I rigged up an instrument hastily and pulled a strip of paper through it, at the same time shouting 'Hallo!' Then the paper was pulled through again, my friend Batchelor and I listening breathlessly.   We heard a distinct sound, which a strong imagination might have

[17] Meumann, Ernst, *Vorlesungen zur Einführung in die Experimentelle Pädagogik,* Ch. XII.   Burgerstein, Leo, und Netolitzky, August, *Handbuch der Schulhygiene,* 454–492.   O'Shea, M. V., *Dynamic Factors in Education,* Ch. XIII.   Warner, Francis, *The Study of Children,* Ch. VII.

translated into the original 'Hallo.' That was enough to lead me to further experiment.—Edison and the phonograph in P. G. Hubert, *Inventors, 237*.

In the amphitheatre were men who had raised their arms and remained in that posture. Sweat covered the faces of others, as if they themselves were struggling with the beast. In the Circus nothing was heard save the sound of flame in the lamps, and the crackle of bits of coal as they dropped from the torches. Their voices died on the lips of the spectators, but their hearts were beating in their breasts as if to split them. It seemed to all that the struggle was lasting for ages. But the man and the beast continued on in their monstrous exertion; one might have said that they were planted in the earth. —*Quo Vadis*, Henry Sienkiewicz, Eng. tr. by J Curtin, 499.

(b) *Experimental.*

Catch yourself during a moment of intense study. Note difference from normal breathing. Note the respiration of others during profound attention. Count the inspirations and expirations for a set time and compare with the normal.

Place the finger on the wrist of a subject and feel the pulse. Tell him to think of one of five objects before him. Name each one, one at a time. Feel the difference in the pulse when the right one is named. Tell the subject to think of some exciting incident in his life, or refer him to one. Note the difference in the pulse.

If laboratory apparatus is accessible, repeat the tests of MacDougall, McGamble, Mentz, Zoneff and Meumann, or others.

2. SENSORY.

(a) *Literary.*

Cyrus opened a door and entered as it were an enormous chamber, but low and dark, for the light came in only through grated openings which separated it from the arena. At first Vinicius could see nothing; he heard only the murmur of voices in the room, and the shouts of people in the amphitheatre. But after a time, when his eyes had grown used to the gloom, he saw crowds of strange beings, resembling wolves and bears. Those were Christians sewed up in skins of beasts.—*Quo Vadis*, H. Sienkiewicz, 421.

> Prithee, see there! behold! look! lo! how say you?
> Why, what care I? If thou canst nod, speak too.
> If charnel-houses and our graves must send
> Those that we bury back, our monuments
> Shall be the maws of kites. (*Ghost vanishes*)
> *Macbeth,* III:iv.

(b) *Experimental.*

Observe the size of the pupil of the eye by means of a mirror. Move slowly towards a light and observe changes in size. Move slowly away from the light towards a darker place, and note changes in size.

Hold some object, as a pencil, at arm's length and fixate some point on it. Move it slowly in the direction of the face till it touches the nose. Note the strain of fixation.

Observe the expression of a nearsighted pupil who is seated too far from the blackboard. Note the peculiar expression of the eyes. Compare the strained look with that of a normal child.

Note the movements of the head when one is listening intently to a sound. Observe the positions of individuals in an audience who are attending to a preacher, a speaker, an actor, etc. Note the lapses when the attention is not held. Note the changes in position when some more stimulating appeal seems to be made.

Take any text and mark letters with crosses, circles, etc., about one inch apart. Vary the spaces making them three quarters of an inch, an inch and a half, etc. See whether or not the eye movements are aided. Note the effect of meaning on the eye pause. Use red ink and compare its efficacy with black ink.[18]

3. MOTOR.

(a) *Literary*.

'France and Liege, and long live the gallant archer! We will live and die with him!'

William de la Marck's eyes sparkled, and he grasped his dagger as if about to launch it at the heart of the audacious speaker; but glancing his eye around, he read something in the looks of his soldiers, which even *he* was obliged to respect.—*Quentin Durward*, Ch. XXII.

[18] Huey, E. B., *Psych. and Ped. of Read.*, 176.

The fruit was standing in the pantry, which by a lattice at a considerable height received light from the kitchen. One day, being alone in the house, I climbed up to see these precious apples. I fetched the spit— tried if it would reach them—it was too short—I lengthened it with a small one which was used for game—my master being very fond of hunting, darted at them several times without success; at length was more fortunate; being transported to find I was bringing up an apple, I drew it gently to the lattice—was going to seize it when (who can express my grief and astonishment!) I found it would not pass through—it was too large. I tried every expedient to accomplish my design, sought supporters to keep the spits in the same position, a knife to divide the apple, and a lath to hold it with; at length, I so far succeeded as to effect the division, and made no doubt of drawing the pieces through; but it was scarcely separated, (compassionate reader, sympathise with my affliction) when both pieces fell into the pantry. The next day (a fine opportunity offering) I renew the trial. I fasten the spits together; get on the stool; take aim; am just going to dart at my prey—unfortunately the dragon did not sleep; the pantry door opens, my master makes his appearance, and, looking up, exclaims, "Bravo!"—*Confessions of Rousseau*, Eng. tr., p. 29.

(b) *Experimental.*

Keep a record of motor diffusions and automatisms made by others. Record your own automatism. Tell what activities they accompany.   Are any automatisms characteristic?

Repeat Jastrow's experiment.

Repeat Campbell and Münsterberg's experiment.

In the following figure, move the eye from *a* to *b*. How does the figure appear?   Move the eye from *c* to *d*. Is there any difference in the appearance of the figure?

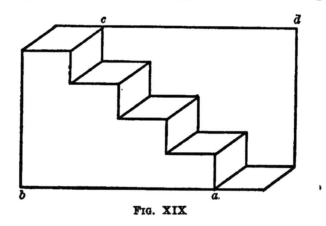

FIG. XIX

Close your eyes.   Try to picture a chariot race, with one in the lead, and one close behind.   Note the movements of the horses, the driver, and the wheels of the chariot.   Are there any eye movements or innervations? Is there any tendency to move the eye from one side to the other in picturing the chariot in the rear?   Are there any other innervations?

Think intensely of the working of any machine with which you are familiar.   Can you picture the motion of rollers, wheels, levers, etc.?   Close your eyes, try to imagine yourself working at it.   Do you feel any motor tendencies?   Localise them.   Refer them to the mental picture. Are they connected with any verbal images or innervations? To what extent do words enter in the motor process? What other parts of the body are affected?

Try to get the meaning of the following:

Since $\Phi(z)$ is uniform, an irreducible infinity of degree n for $\Phi(z)$ is an irreducible infinity of degree $n+1$ for $\Phi'(z)$. Moreover $\Phi'(z)$, being uniform, has no infinity which is not an infinity of $\Phi(z)$; thus the order of $\Phi'(z)$ is $\Sigma(n+1)$, or its order is greater than that of $\Phi(z)$ by an integer which represents the number of distinct irreducible infinities of $\Phi(z)$, no account being taken of their degree. If, then, a function be of the order m, the order of its derivative is not less than $m+1$ and is not greater than $2m$. Forsyth, A. R., *Theory of Functions of a Complex Variable*, 258.

Read this over carefully. Try to get the connection. Do you feel any strain? Localise it. Are there any motor tendencies? Is there any articulatory accompaniment?

4. FATIGUE.

(a) *Literary*.

How deadly tired I was in those days I do not think I myself knew until I went to Boston one evening to help discuss sweating at the Institute of Technology. I had an hour to spare, and went around into Beacon Street to call upon a friend. I walked mechanically up the stoop and rang the bell. My friend was not in, said the servant who came to the door. Who should she say called? I stood and looked at her like a fool; I had forgotten my name. . . . Until I actually read my name on my card it was as utterly gone as if I had never heard it.—Riis, J. A., *The Making of an American*, 306.

For eight years I taught in public elementary day schools in a cotton town, and in all the schools in which I was a teacher, there was a great proportion of factory children—I have seen them fall asleep over their lesson-books or tasks, after they have been in the factory all the morning (six hours).—Clarke, A., *The Effects of the Factory System*, 97.

(b) Experimental.

Mark *a*'s for an hour in the morning, and for an hour when you are tired, late at night, after heavy work, etc. Note the difference in the amount and in the error.

Note the feeling which accompanies fatigue. Localise it if possible. Try to intensify the feeling by straining the muscles in the area involved, by wrinkling the forehead intensely, etc.

Can you distinguish drowsiness from fatigue, or lack of interest, or unwillingness to do the work, from fatigue? What conditions operate in fatigue which are not present in the other states?

§ III. DEVELOPMENT

Of the physiological constituents of the attentive process the organic and the sensory are more or less instinctive and so do not involve

11

much development. The motor, on the other hand, goes through a number of stages of development.

1. MOTOR. Movements may be (1) reflex, or instinctive, (2) ideomotor, or (3) voluntary.

(*a*) *Instinctive.* In instinctive or primitive attention a stimulus calls forth a motor response without further thought on the part of the individual. The sensorimotor process is realised automatically by virtue of the inherent nature of the nervous system. A reflex differs from an instinctive movement in that the former is simple in character and usually consists of a single movement, as, the winking of an eyelash, or sneezing. An instinct, however, consists of a series of coördinated movements which involve a larger area. A sudden sound, for example, may cause a child to turn, lift its hands, and run without. The whole process is realised in a purely automatic manner.[19]

(*b*) *Ideomotor.* Such instinctive movements leave motor traces which facilitate further action and control. Moreover, the movements them-

[19] See Morgan, C. Lloyd, *Habit and Instinct.* Kirkpatrick, E. A., *Fundamentals of Child Study.* Hobhouse, L. T., *Mind in Evolution*, Chs. III, IV. Darwin, C., *The Descent of Man*, Chs. II, III. Loeb, J., *Comp. Phys. of the Br. and Comp. Psych.*, Ch. XIII. Baldwin, J. M., *Development and Evolution*, Chs. V, VI. James, W., *Princ. of Psych.*, Ch. XXIV.

selves become connected in a more or less definite manner with situations both real and ideal. The instinctive responses become more accurate and refined.[20]   Any unnecessary movements which do not give pleasure or satisfaction fall away through a lack of such stimuli as impel repetition.   The selected responses on the other hand become closely bound with impressions, images, and ideas.   When attention is directed to a situation which is more familiar, the mere impression or idea results in a series of coördinated movements which effect a definite purpose with comparatively little waste.   In such a case the action is ideomotor.   No consciousness of the act as such is involved.   Simply the situation alone, as impression, image, or what not, excites proper motor coördination and control.   Common examples are those situations in which revived series of images call forth a series of unconscious acts on our part.   In attending to some object, for instance, we unconsciously place it in a certain position, get material to fix it, if necessary, and the like.   In attention to some ideal situation, as the thought of a book, or the image of a picture, one similarly feels impelled

[20] See Thorndike, E. L., *Animal Intelligence.*

to go for the book, look at the picture, ask for it, and so on.[21]

(c) *Voluntary*. When there is conscious selection of a movement, when an idea or image strongly impels action as preferential to other possible actions, when conscious choice is involved, the control is voluntary. On the ideal side there are usually deliberation and selection as already explained. On the motor side there is either an image of some action or a series of motor innervations and tendencies due to the dominance of an image or idea. When the situation to be realised is remote, the motor control becomes centred in a series of means. When the means have been worked out ideally and a course of action has been selected, the process of realisation goes ahead almost automatically. The situation in question is fixated and the various aspects call forth motor responses of the kind which have been selected. In the choice of any series of actions, the general tendency and direction alone seem to be involved. Any further amplification and refinement become effected only when the actual process of control is under way. Further deliberation and choice may at

[21] James, W., *Princ.*, Ch. XXVI. Baldwin, J. M., *Ment. Dev.*, Pt. III.

time halt the process of control whenever such amplification becomes necessary. One who is seeking means to improve his work, who is confronted with a new problem, who is placed in a predicament, and the like, must select ways and means, try them, correct his errors, think out new plans, apply them, compare the results with previous efforts, and the like. The sensory and the motor intermingle, one reinforcing the other.[22]

In the order of acquisition, random movements precede the more coördinated and these are followed by selected and serial adjustments. In pathological conditions, however, a reverse order seems to be emphasised. The voluntary coördinations, such as are found in speaking and writing, are lost first. Then come such stages as partial ataxia, rhythmic deafness, and general ataxia.

The general order of sensorimotor development is indicated in the following table:[28]

[22] See Woodworth, R. S., 'The Accuracy of a Voluntary Movement,' *Psych. Rev., Mon. Sup.*, 3:Pts. VII, VIII. Münsterberg, H., *Grundzüge der Psychologie*, 1:Ch. XV. Stout, G. F., *Man. of Psych.*, Bk. IV, Ch. X.

[28] Baldwin, J. M., *Ment. Dev.*, Third ed., 390.

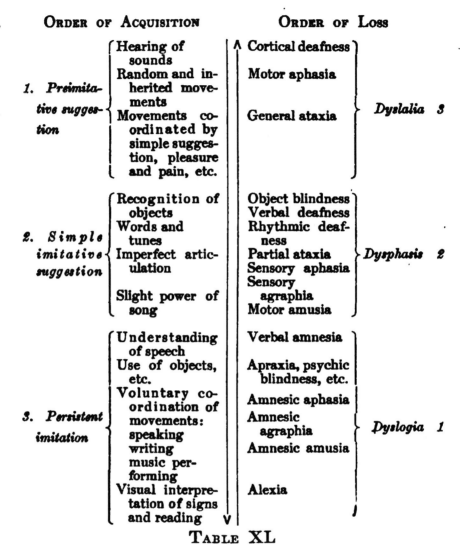

ORDER OF ACQUISITION	ORDER OF LOSS	
1. *Preimitative suggestion* — Hearing of sounds; Random and inherited movements; Movements co-ordinated by simple suggestion, pleasure and pain, etc.	Cortical deafness; Motor aphasia; General ataxia	*Dyslalia 3*
2. *Simple imitative suggestion* — Recognition of objects; Words and tunes; Imperfect articulation; Slight power of song	Object blindness; Verbal deafness; Rhythmic deafness; Partial ataxia; Sensory aphasia; Sensory agraphia; Motor amusia	*Dysphasis 2*
3. *Persistent imitation* — Understanding of speech; Use of objects, etc.; Voluntary co-ordination of movements: speaking, writing, music performing; Visual interpretation of signs and reading	Verbal amnesia; Apraxia, psychic blindness, etc.; Amnesic aphasia; Amnesic agraphia; Amnesic amusia; Alexia	*Dyslogia 1*

TABLE XL

§ IV. EXPLANATION

1. ORGANIC. The changes in respiration which form a part of the attentive process are due in part to the localisation of control and to the inhibition thereby necessary. Those parts of the organism which are not called into play need not function so vigorously, and so do not necessi-

tate the usual respiration.   This is especially true
in the case of mental application and in many of
the laboratory tests which involve visual fixation,
tactile reaction, and the like.   Moreover, breathing may, by becoming too prominent, form a
center of attention in itself or interfere with concentration to other aspects of the situation.
Vasoconstriction, changes in pulse, etc., like
other biological aspects can not yet be fully explained.   With respect to attention, however, it
is highly probable that such changes are necessary whenever effort becomes localised.   The
general tonicity of the system loses its more or
less uniform character and becomes emphasised
in those portions of the organism which are
called actively into play.   Increased demands by
one part of the system necessitate some depletion in other parts.   This is probably effected by
vasoconstriction and other changes.

2. SENSORY.   The function of the sensory
adjustments in the process of attention is the
fixation of the situation in the field of clearness
and distinctness.   The adaptations and instinctive changes in the end organs facilitate the
reception of impressions while the motor accommodations and movements serve to select aspects
of the given field and to bring them out more

distinctly and clearly. When such fixation is accomplished more accurate and refined control becomes possible.

3. MOTOR. Motor adjustments and attitudes are essential in attention, not only to give greater distinctness and clearness, but, in more ideal processes, to indicate meaning and direction to the ideas and images which arise. The function of the motor attitude in meaning tends to be overlooked because it is so closely connected with the impression or image, and because it often exists only as a tendency. But without the motor attitude the visual or other image or impression would have little distinctive meaning. Visual differences aid in reviving such characteristic motor tendencies, but in themselves are no guarantee for any specific signification. This is shown in the early stages of a child's development and in pathological cases of apraxia.

The fact that the child emphasises use and motor response in his definitions leads one to attribute the meaning and signification of objects and words to motor attitudes and tendencies. In a *Boy's Dictionary* of 215 words compiled by F. E. Wolff, the following definitions are given:[24]

[24] See Chamberlain, A. F., *The Child*, 146.

Kiss is if you hug and kiss somebody.
Mast is what holds the sail on top of a ship.
Nail is something to put things together.
Quarrel is if you begin a little fight.
Ring is what you wear on your finger.

Binet obtained a similar series as shown in the following:[25]

A knife is something which cuts.
Water is something to drink.
A hat is something to put on the head.
A box is to put things into.
A piece of sugar is to eat.

It is of interest to note that Webster in his *Dictionary* emphasises use and function to almost the same extent as do children.[26]

Even in adult consciousness there seems to be nothing inherent in a visual situation as such which gives it a distinctive meaning. Why one object should be called 'Pie,' and eaten, and another 'Cover,' and placed on a bowl is not evident from the appearance of each, in itself. Only by a process of motor experience does each acquire a meaning. Similarly, 'Come,' and 'Go' have nothing in them as mere sounds to indicate actions peculiar to each. Sweet points out the fact

[25] Binet, Alfred, 'Perceptions d'Enfants,' *Rev. Phil.*, 30:582-611.
[26] See Barnes, 'A Study of Children's Interests,' *Studies in Education*, Ed. by Earl Barnes.

that for some Germans the sound 'het,' stands
for 'head,' 'hat,' and 'had.' Meaning in each of
these three cases can not be due to the sound as
such but must be accompanied in part by the
motor attitude. In apraxia a loss of meaning is
seen by the confusion which arises when a patient
seeks to use objects. The visual situation is
present but it seems to have no special signification for the patient. One object is used for
another.

The patient will put his breeches on one shoulder and
his hat upon the other, will bite into the soap and lay
his shoes on the table, or take his food into his hand
and throw it down again, not knowing what to do with
it, etc.[27]

The diffusions and innervations which are present in attention to ideas or images probably
serve to give meaning to the otherwise barren
representations. By giving meaning, such motor
attitudes serve to give direction and associative
impulsion, for without meaning, one series of
ideas would do just as well as another. Added
vividness likewise results because of the motor
attitude.

In processes of deliberation which result in
decision but no immediate action, it is the motor

[27] James, W., *Princ.*, 1:52.

attitude which determines selection and choice.
Complete reaction may be unnecessary to decide
whether or not one series of ideas or the other
will result in satisfaction or pleasure, and the
motor attitude takes its place. According as
experience is more or less thorough and extensive
will such attitude prove true. When an attitude
is misleading, we call the judgment or the decision false, *i.e.*, if the attitude were fully realised,
the actual manipulation and control would not
effect what the attitude signified. None the less,
whether right or wrong, the attitude is the determining factor in such ideal deliberation. The
motor attitude becomes especially prominent in
cases of conflict. When the smooth flow of
thought, or the even rhythm of reading is blocked
by a strange idea or expression which interferes
with further interpretation and appreciation, a
disturbance arises which manifests itself in motor
expression of some sort. Such excitement may
become extremely marked. It may develop into
actual movement, or it may end in explosive
expression.[28]

4. FATIGUE. In the metabolic changes due to
sensorimotor activity waste products are found.
In muscular work it has been established that

[28] See Sidis, Boris, *Psychopathological Researches*, Ch. VI.

CO_2 is generated from the oxidisation of some of carbon constituents of the muscle. The glycogen gradually disappears. Sarcolactic acid likewise accumulates.[29] When there is an excess of sarcolactic acid and acid potassium phosphate in the muscle it loses its irritability and contractility. It is less easily stimulated. It responds less easily in an accurate and determinate manner, in other words, it is physiologically fatigued. If the fatigue becomes too great there may follow a total lack of response to stimulation. It is evident that as fast as waste products are formed the muscle loses in material by this process of decomposition. This also tends to interfere with the muscle response.

The location of the physiological effect of fatigue is not in the muscle directly. By experiment fatigue has been found to operate in the motor plates. If, for example, one voluntarily lifts a weight or pulls a spring with the finger till fatigue prevents further response by such central stimulation, the finger will still respond to direct electrical stimulation, *i.e.*, the muscle will contract in response to the electric stimulation. As the nerve fibre can not be perceptibly fatigued, only the motor end plates remain as

[29] Howell, W. H., *Phys.*, Ch. II.

the seat of fatigue. So, too, if a nerve is electrically stimulated till no further muscle response is possible, the muscle will respond when directly stimulated. By elimination, the end plates remain.[30] Finally, if a muscle is placed in a glass of curare, no contraction will be effected if the nerve is stimulated, while direction stimulation of the muscle will still be effective. In this case the poison acts on the motor end plates.[31]

The changes which go on in the cortex are not so clearly known. Various facts, however, lead one to suppose that metabolic changes of some kind go on in the brain. Mosso, for example, found an increase in temperature in the brain correspondent with heightened mental activity. Since heat is the result of chemical change it is probable that some metabolism goes on in such a case. Hodge showed that in the case of the sparrow the spinal ganglion cells were shrunken at the end of the day and fuller after a night's rest. Waller offers the following series of tests: If the gastrocnemius or leg muscle of a frog is excited by electric stimulation of the brain and

[30] Waller, A. D., *Phys.*, Ch. X.

[31] *Practical Physiology*, by A. P. Beddard, L. Hill, J. S. Edkins, and J. J. R. Macleod, Ch. IX.

bulb till it no longer responds, it can still be excited by direct stimulation of the sciatic nerve. When such stimulation fails to excite response, a third series of contractions can be effected by means of direct excitation of the muscle. The fatigue in the first instance is probably conditioned by cerebral factors. Whether there is a less ready response within the cell itself, or whether the seat lies in the connections between the cell and the neurons, or what the process is, has not been determined. Connected with the whole process is probably the devitalised condition of the blood through the fatigue by-products.

The external conditions which produce fatigue are well known. Any thing which gives rise to the intrinsic conditions discussed in the above paragraph will cause fatigue. Excessive stimulation of some organ, muscle, etc., without intervals for recuperation will bring about fatigue. A lack of rest will have a similar effect. Predisposing conditions are a lack of proper nourishment, insufficient oxygination of the blood, or devitalisation through sickness, poison, shock, etc. Such conditions will render normal exertions fatiguing.

In mental application it might seem that the

muscles are not called into any activity of account. Simple inhibition of movement, however, is a considerable strain and calls the muscles into play just as does more expressive action.[32] The more active innervations and motor attitudes, their constant changing and shifting as the series of ideas change, the motor diffusions, and the like also deplete motor energy to a considerable extent.

[32] *Yale Psych. Stud., Psych. Rev., Mon. Sup.,* 7:141-184, 'Analysis of Reaction Movements,' by C. H. Judd, C. N. McAllister, and W. M. Steele.

CHAPTER V

RECAPITULATION

§ I. DEFINITION OF ATTENTION

Attention must be considered from two points of view, (1) the sensory or ideal and (2) the motor or physiological. Without the other, either is more or less empty and meaningless. The result of the sensorimotor control is distinctness and clearness within the given field. Considering these aspects, we may define attention thus:

Attention is a process of sensorimotor control which tends to increase the clearness and distinctness of the given field.

§ II. OUTLINE OF ASPECTS

We have then two aspects of attention, the subjective and the objective. The subjective aspect includes the sensory (ideal) and the motor (physiological) processes. The objective aspect includes both qualitative and quantitative changes. Under the former we have clearness and distinctness. Under the latter we have the size of the field of attention, the fluctuation of minimal stimuli, and facilitation or arrest of the parts of the field in their temporal or spatial relations. In outline form the subjective process and the objective effects may be given as follows:

Subjective	Objective
Motor (physiological)	Qualitative
Organic	Clearness
Respiration	Distinctness
Vasoconstriction	Persistence
Circulation	Quantitative
Sensory	Fluctuation
Accommodation	Unity
Fixation	Facilitation
Motor	Arrest
Diffusion	
Innervation	
Full control	
Sensory (ideal)	
Fusion, etc.	
Free association	
Deliberation	

§ III. Outline of Stages

The stages of attention may be outlined as follows:

Primary	Assimilative
Sense stimulation	Sense stimulation plus ideal reinforcement
Instinctive motor response with waste	Motor control through unconscious action and habit
Lack of definite direction (residual bases formed)	Direction still external

Secondary
    Definite guidance by images or ideas
    Construction of a means cognised as such
    Persistence of the means by association with
        an end
    Direction internal

§ IV. OUTLINE OF CONDITIONS

Objective conditions which tend to impel attention are:

> *Difference*
>   Quality
>   Intensity
>   (Extensity)
> *Change*
>   Quality
>   Intensity
>   (Extensity)
> *Pleasure-pain*
> *Time*

Subjective conditions which facilitate persistence of attention are:

> *Preadjustment*
> *Reinforcement*
> *Practice*
> *Pause* (*rest*)
> *Natural vitality*
> *Mental ability*[1]

[1] Compare the discussions in: Pillsbury, W. B., *Attention.*
Titchener, E. B., *The Psychology of Feeling and Attention.*
Roerich, Edouard, *L'Attention Spontanée et Volontaire.* Nayrac,

Jean-Paul, *Physiologie et Psychologie de l'Attention.* Serol, M., 'Analyse de l'Attention,' *Rev. de Phil.,* 7:597-620 (Rev. in *Psych. Bul.,* 3:140-143). McDougall, W., 'The Physiological Factors of the Attention-Process,' *Mind,* 11:316-351, 12:289-302, and 473-488. Kohn, H. E., 'Zur Theorie de Aufmerksamkeit,' *Abhand. z. Phil. u. ihrer Gesch.,* 5. Shand, A. F., 'An Analysis of Attention,' *Mind,* 3:449-473, and 'Attention and Will,' *Mind,* 4:450-471. Bradley, F. H., 'On Active Attention,' *Mind,* 11:1-30, and 'Is There Any Special Activity of Attention?' *Mind,* 11:305-323. Calkins, M. W., *An Int. to Psych.,* 'Appendix,' Sect. VII.

PART II
INTEREST

Part II
Interest

CHAPTER VI
THE MOTOR ASPECT OF INTEREST

§ I. DESCRIPTION

On its motor side, interest is essentially a striving, a conation, an appetition, a tendency towards something. An attitude is taken towards a situation, an impulsion is felt, a desire to come into closer relationship with an object is present. Between the subject and the object there is an unrealised condition felt in its motor aspect as a strain, a stress, a moment of tendency towards further control. One is interested, for example, in some object in a show window, a tennis racket, book, or what not. One feels, or has, or takes an interest in the object. The 'feel' of the interest, its existence as a psychological fact is dependent upon the motor attitude which the object in question calls forth. Motor tendencies or incipient movements are excited by the object, a general attitude towards it is taken, a certain anticipation is aroused. This attitude may be felt as a general restlessness, a motor 'set,' or at times as a general thrill. If further contact with the stimulating object is possible, this motor attitude may become more explicit in a series of actual movements and manipulations. The interest which a child shows for a toy emphasises this motor aspect. With young children who have less control over their actions there are movements of the hands, face and body. Sometimes there are little cries of glee or other expressions to indicate the direction which the interest has taken. When the object is under the child's control the motor tendencies become more or less manifest in a number of actions, manipulations, and attempts at control of the object.

Where interest is felt in some ideal situation, as in a story, a problem, etc., the motor tendencies are not so evident. Over and above the attitude which gives meaning to the situation in the center of attention are those tendencies which impel one to hurry on to the end, to reach the climax, to work out the solution, to facilitate fuller control of the object in question, and the like. Sometimes the motor attitude becomes so strong that it overrides normal realisation and seeks to avoid the more gradual control which will lead to the desired end. The individual will then turn to the end of the book to see how the story ends, or will go to a 'Key' to find the solution of his problem, or will seek others to get further information and help.

The motor aspect of interest is essentially teleological, end-seeking. It points ahead and to the future. One feels interest in a situation in that the situation excites innervations and tendencies, which, when more fully realised, will bring about a condition of pleasure, ease, satisfaction, and the like. A child has an interest in a toy, for example, and realises that interest when his manipulations and control bring about a condition of rest, ease, satisfaction, or pleasure. In so far as the future moment is realised will the interest continue. Should there be a check or disappointment, the interest will wane. Thus, the child may find the toy not to his liking, or perhaps painful and dissatisfying. His interest in it will then be less intense upon another occasion. Even if the object itself is only an indirect means to the realisation of a future moment, it will, on that account, impel interest, and excite tendencies towards fuller control. A factory girl, for example, can hardly be said to have any interest in the rolling of cigars, as such. But in so far as she gets twenty five cents a hundred, will her interest hold in the process to the extent of making five or six hundred a day. The prospective situation impels control of present conditions, even though these conditions are more or less disagreeable.

Interest, as thus described, is not a feeling of pleasure, ease, satisfaction, quiescence, or what not. In themselves, such feelings are passive and lack the dynamic aspect characteristic of interest. Interest is dynamic, it points ahead, it is a form of striving, of motor impulsion, and is felt as a conation or motor attitude. Feeling of pleasure, satisfaction, etc., is of a more passive nature. As felt it lies enmeshed in the present. One who is enjoying the taste of fruit, or the fragrance of a flower, or the esthetic satisfaction arising from the contemplation of a painting or a statue, feels pleasure, and this pleasure exists in the present. One may lean back, as it were, and absorb it. If such satisfaction or pleasure, however, is not present, and is possible only through control of some situation in the center of attention, an interest in the situation will exist and will rouse motor attitudes and tendencies. These tendencies are felt as interest and guide further manipulation. One may, for example, see a picture for sale, and be excited to the extent of asking the price of it, and of making arrangements to buy it. One does not then lean back, but becomes active, or feels impelled so to do.[1]

In so far as interest points ahead, it has some more or less definite object in view. Aspects of a situation come to have a value to the individual to a great extent because of the tendencies and attitudes which they are able to arouse. This psychological phase of interest must be considered in any economic treatment of value. No doubt the amount of labor which is put into an object will condition, in part, the value which such an object possesses. So, too, will the amount of the material available, the supply of articles at hand, and the like, affect value. An

[1] Compare the descriptions of interest in: Volkmann, Wilhelm, *Lehrbuch der Psychologie*, 2:206, 207. Stumpf, Carl, *Tonpsychologie*, 1:68, 69, and 2:279-280. Baldwin, J. M., *Handbook of Psychology*, 'Feeling and Will,' 139-146, and Ch. VII. Sully, J., *The Human Mind*, 1:163. Stout, G. F., *Analytic Psychology*, 1:224-225, and Bk. II, Ch. III. Calkins, M. W., *Introduction to Psychology*, 137, 140, 488. Titchener, E. B., *The Psychology of Feeling and Attention*, and *Out. of Psych.*, (New revision). Dewey, J., 'Interest as Related to Will,' *Sec. Sup. to the Her. Yearbook*, 1903. Related treatments from the standpoint of 'value' will be found in: Ehrenfels, Christian von, *System der Werttheorie*, 1, 'Psychologie des Begehrens.' Kriebig, Josef Clemens, *Psychologische Grundlegung eines Systems der Werttheorie*. Meinong, Alexius von, *Psychologischethische Untersuchungen zur Werttheorie*. Münsterberg, H., *Philosophie der Werte*. Lipps, Theodor, *Vom Fühlen, Wollen und Denken*.

important aspect, however, in the determination of the value of an object, is the motor attitude which it is able to arouse, the tendencies to possess it which the object can excite, in short, the interest which it possesses for the consumer.[2]

According to the relation in which an interest-exciting situation stands to the individual, we may, on the motor side, distinguish at least three forms of interest, namely, curiosity, expectation, and desire.

Curiosity, expectation and desire. When a situation is partly known and partly unknown, the known aspects excite motor tendencies along grooves which have been formed by previous experience. The known elements may have been experienced in a form similar to that in which they are in the partially known situation, or they may have been combined in a different manner or with different situations. They excite an attitude which may or may not be fit for the new situation. In so far as aspects of the situation are not known, they impel innervations and tendencies towards a further control which will dispel the uncertainty which is aroused, and

[2] See Jevons, W. S., *The Theory of Political Economy*, Ch. III. Wieser, Friedrich von, *Natural Value*, Eng. tr. by C. A. Malloch. Clark, John Bates, *The Distribution of Wealth*. Compare the discussions in Adam Smith, David Ricardo, Karl Marx, etc.

which will produce a feeling of rest and quiescence. Such attitudes and tendencies are felt as interest.

When a situation is not immediately present but is awaited with feelings of strain, tension, and sometimes with anxiety, we have the interest of expectation. The situation in question is more or less fully known, but immediate control is not possible because the situation is not present. Control can not be realised. Tendencies to such control, however, are present, and it is the attitude taken with reference to the situation which is to come which constitutes the basis of the interest. Since reaction is impossible, only the motor 'set' can be present.

A strong form of interest is conscious desire. Not only is there a prospective situation or terminus to which the individual takes an attitude, but, in addition, such attitude stimulates him to further effort, and excites tendencies towards a control of the present which will lead to the end desired. If such means are not actively sought, desire may lapse into mere wish. One may wish for the pot of gold at the other end of the rainbow, for example, but one actively desires control of an object, in that one works in the present, removes obstacles, seeks aid, and the like, so as to reach the coveted situation. The motor tendencies and innervations which are felt to control a present means which will lead to the end are felt as desire and constitute the motor aspect of the interest.

A few points of difference between these three forms of interest may be noted. Expectation and desire both have reference to some prospective situation. The former, however, is a more passive state. In expectation, realisation is dependent either upon the activity or lack of activity of some one else, or upon external conditions which seem out of the individual's control. Time, or change in extrinsic conditions, or action on the part of another is what separates the interested person from the state towards which he is looking. He can do little on his own account to further realisation of the situation which he wants. He feels tendencies, however, which are excited by the anticipation of this situation, and so feels an interest in it. In active desire, on the other hand, means are sought with a view of coming into closer contact with the situation desired. The individual begins to work out his general attitude into a series of definite reactions. He bends the present towards the future and reconstructs what is under his immediate control for the purpose of realising some prospective moment. Curiosity differs from both desire and expectation in that the situation which excites it is present and under control of the individual concerned. In so far as it is partially unknown, its full significance remains in doubt. There is, however, a definite starting point from which further reaction and control may begin. In expectation and desire the situation is remote and out of the individual's immediate control.[3]

§ II. ILLUSTRATION

1. LITERARY.

Compare the states of mind indicated by the following selections from Tennyson:

> How dull it is to pause, to make an end,
> To rust unburnish'd, not to shine in use!
> As tho' to breathe were life. Life piled on life
> Were all too little, and of one to me
> Little remains: but every hour is saved
> From that eternal silence, something more,
> A bringer of new things: and vile it were
> For some three suns to store and hoard myself,
> And this gray spirit yearning in desire
> To follow knowledge like a sinking star,
> Beyond the utmost bound of human thought.
>
> *Ulysses*, by Tennyson.

[3] See Arnold, F., 'The Psychology of Interest,' *Psych. Rev.*, 13: 221-238, and 291-315, and 'Interest and Attention,' *Psych. Bul.*, 2: 361-368.

They sat them down upon the yellow sand,
Between the sun and moon upon the shore;
And sweet it was to dream of Fatherland,
Of child and wife, and slave; but evermore
Most weary seem'd the sea, weary the oar,
Weary the wandering fields of barren foam.
Then some one said, "We will return no more";
And all at once they sang, "Our island home
Is far beyond the wave; we will no longer roam."
The Lotus-Eaters, by Tennyson.

Contrast the two states of mind with reference to (1) the motor tendencies, (2) the nature of the situations which control action, (3) the future reference of each, and (4) the passivity of the feelings of rest and quiescence.

"And now," said she, "we have to get the key of *that;* and who's to touch it, I should like to know!" . . .

I felt in his pockets, one after another. A few small coins, a thimble, and some thread and big needles, a piece of pigtail tobacco bitten away at the end, his gully with the crooked handle, a pocket compass, and a tinder box, were all that they contained, and I began to despair.

"Perhaps it's round his neck," suggested my mother.

Overcoming a strong repugnance, I tore open his shirt at the neck, and there, sure enough, hanging to a bit of tarry string, we found the key. At this triumph we were filled with hope, and hurried up-stairs, without delay, to the little room where he had slept so long, and where his box had stood since the day of his arrival. . . .

"Give me the key," said my mother: and though the lock was very stiff, she had turned it and thrown back the lid in a twinkling.—*Treasure Island*, by Stevenson, *32*.

Are there any repelling elements in the search? Why does it continue? Does the interest inhere in the key as such? What is the end to be realised?

Here I sit at the desk again, watching his eye— humbly watching his eye, as he rules a ciphering-book for another victim whose hands have just been flattened by that identical ruler, and who is trying to wipe the sting out with a pocket-handkerchief. I have plenty to do. I don't watch his eye in idleness, but because I am morbidly attracted to it, in a dread desire to know what he will do next, and whether it will be my turn to suffer, or somebody else's. A lane of boys beyond me, with the same interest in his eye, watch it too.—*David Copperfield*. Dickens. Ch. VII.

2. EXPERIMENTAL.

Note the attitude of a child who is interested in a toy, a book, etc. Mark the facial expression, the body posture, the finger movements, etc.

Watch a child who is reading what seems to be an interesting book. Note movements of anticipation, excitement, anxiety to get ahead in the story.

When you are explaining something to a learner, note

13

your own tendencies to do the work yourself instead of letting the learner do it.

Try to examine your own attitude when you are interested in an object, in a story, in the solution of a problem, etc. Note feelings of stress, of motor tendencies, and the like.

Read the following: Then there came a single call on the sea-pipe, and that was the signal. A knot of them made one rush of it, cutlass in hand, against the door; and at the same moment, the glass of the skylight was dashed in a thousand pieces, and a man leaped through and landed on the floor. Before he got to his feet, I had clapped a pistol to his back, and . . . — *Kidnapped.* Stevenson. 94.

Do you note any feelings of unrest, of desire to continue, of motor innervations towards readjustment, or the like? What is the aim of the publisher of a serial story who ends part of a chapter with, 'To be continued in our next?'

§ III. DEVELOPMENT

The rise of interest is dependent chiefly upon two factors, (1) pleasure-pain, etc., and (2) instinct. When any situation excites pleasure-pain, etc., it is a means of stimulating reaction. Such pleasure-pain, etc., however, is not the interest which it develops. In connection with instinctive behavior it affords a basis for the development of interest. The process is some-

what as follows: Any situation which excites
feelings of shock, pleasure, satisfaction, pain,
and the like, other things being equal, will arouse
reaction and attention to it. If such a situation,
after it has entered the center of the field of
attention, persists in the focus, and leads to a
pleasing or satisfying terminus, traces of the
impressions, reactions, etc., are left in the individual who is attending. As the result of the
control, residual traces, visual, motor, and the
like, remain. The situation has then a meaning,
and, in addition, points to a repetition of the
terminus which is known to be pleasing or satisfying. When this situation or one like it is
again before the individual, in addition to inherent impelling powers of its own, it will tend
to excite an attitude favorable to its persistence
in the focus of attention. The individual will
feel impelled to react towards it, to control it,
to manipulate in the manner which on a former
occasion resulted in feelings of pleasure, ease,
satisfaction, quiescence, and the like. The terminus to which it once led will again be sought.
In other words, the situation has an interest
which excites the individual to maintain it in the
center of attentive control. This interest in an
attitude over and above any feelings of pleasure

which the situation, as such, may be able to excite.

The following account illustrates to some extent this process:

She was holding objects, looking at them, and pulling them about for some moments, before they went to her mouth. . The pleasure of this handling seemed to be in the free movement of the objects (seen and felt at the same time), not especially in the touch sensations. When this new pleasure was exhausted, things went to the mouth as before for the enjoyment of touch. . . . In a few hours the baby was reaching for everything near her, and in three days more her desire to lay hold on things was the dominant motive of her life. Her grasping was still oftener with both hands than one, and was somewhat slow, but always accurate.[4]

The child's desire to get a 'penny' for a stick of candy, his interest in a toy, and the like, are common examples. Until experienced, the candy, toy, etc., mean little. But after the child has eaten the candy, played with the toy, controlled the situation which leads to a pleasing or satisfying terminus, the sight of the candy, toy, or what not, will excite tendencies to control again the object in question. The sight of the object alone may rouse pleasure. In addition are the

[4] Shinn, Milicent Washburn, *The Biography of a Baby*, 142, 143.

revived tendencies to play, manipulate, control, and the like, which have previously resulted in pleasure, etc. At first, instincts and feelings are sufficient to impel attention and stimulate motor control. After the child has reacted there is the resulting residual motor and ideal basis which impels and guides further control. The situation is now one which has interest. It means for the individual the possibility of realising pleasurable, satisfying, quieting feelings, of obtaining joy, ease, satisfaction, and the like. It will, when again presented, excite motor tendencies to play, manipulate, handle, etc., and a desire to control it because of the terminus to which previous control has shown it to lead. Consciousness of this end need not be present in distinct form, but may lie enmeshed in a fringe of meaning.

The motor, visual, tactile, and other impressions will leave traces strong enough to excite interest even when the toy or other object is not before the child. The mere mention of the object, its name, a picture of it, etc., will excite an interest in the individual strong enough to impel attempted control. Verbal and motor expressions usually show the presence of such interest. The motor attitude and innervations which are excited give the feel of interest and stamp the object as one which has a value or worth. In all this, the feeling of interest should not be confused with the more passive feelings of ease, satisfaction, pleasure, or quiescence.

A situation may give rise to pain, dissatisfaction, unrest, etc. In such a case its repetition will also excite interest but of a negative character. Motor tendencies will then point away from the situation. There will be felt innervations and impulses to get away from the disturbing object, remove it, destroy it, or do away with it. Thus Preyer notes:

Screaming when water 26° C. was poured over him in the bath appeared, a few days after the first experiment of this sort, even before the bathing, at sight of the tub, sponge, and water. Previously, fear had only in very rare cases occasioned screaming, now the idea of the cold and wet that were to be expected was enough to occasion violent screaming.[5]

The negative interest which the situation arouses is the feeling of these motor tendencies to react in a manner unfavorable to the persistence of the object in the focus of consciousness. As in the more positive cases of interest, experi-

[5] Preyer, W., *The Development of the Intellect*, Eng. tr. by H. W. Brown, 132.

ence is necessary before the full meaning of the situation can be appreciated.

Primary, secondary and acquired interest. Such interest as is excited by the object itself because of the terminus to which it leads directly may be called a primary interest. In primary interest the object itself is desired and fuller control of it is attempted because of its inherent power to produce pleasurable or satisfying feelings. Should the object be more remote, should direct control of it be impossible, any means which will lead to control of it will have an interest in that they excite tendencies similar to those roused by the situation itself. Thus, if a series of means, *a, b, c, . . .* etc., lead to *A,* interest in *a, b, c, . . .* etc., will be felt because of the connection which they have with *A.* Such interest which is derived from a primary interest may be called a secondary interest.

The nature of secondary interest emphasises the difference between a feeling of interest and feelings of pleasure-pain, satisfaction, and the like. The means, as such, may be highly unpleasant or even painful and repelling, and still may possess a secondary interest because of some pleasing or satisfying terminus to which they lead. A child, for example, may be impelled to work sums in arithmetic, run errands, or do other disagreeable tasks because of the secondary interest which such work possesses. In themselves the means may have little impelling power. But as connected with an end which has primary interest, they are able to excite secondary interest.

Secondary interest with means pleasurable or painful may be represented in the following scheme: Let + indicate means which are pleasing or satisfying in themselves, and — means which are painful or dissatisfying. Both lead to a situation, *P,* which has primary interest. The interest in the means is secondary. In both cases interest is of a positive character in that it leads to a situation which is pleasing or satisfying. The following scheme illustrates this positive movement:

$$S \begin{array}{c} \textit{agreeable} \\ + + + + + \\ \xrightarrow{\quad\quad} \\ - - - - - \\ \textit{disagreeable} \end{array} \; P$$

Negative interest may be represented in a similar manner. In this case the means lead away from a situation which is repelling and which has a negative interest. Interest of such a sort may be represented as follows:

```
              agreeable
          +  +  +  +  +  S
   P                        ———————>
          —  —  —  —  —  S
          disagreeable
```

Comparing positive and negative interests, both primary (P) and secondary (S) with pleasurable ($+$) and painful ($—$) means, we have the following scheme:

```
  ·    S + + + + +      + + + + + S
   ————>          P  P            ————>
       S — — — — —      — ·— — — — — S
          Positive         Negative
```

The distinctions illustrated by this diagram should be clearly kept in mind. Secondary interest is often confused with negative interest, especially in educational theory and practice. Interest in a painful means which leads to something positive is very different from that in a painful means which leads away from a more painful situation, at least as far as the terminus is concerned.

If the means are pleasurable and satisfying an interest will tend to develop in them as such. If the end has sufficient impelling power to hold attention to the means and to excite a secondary interest in them, continued experience which results in pleasure and satisfaction will develop an interest in such means. Such interest may be called an acquired interest. Acquired interest may be developed even in the case of means which at first are repelling and disagreeable. Many of our interests in later life are of such a character. A child is not born a developed mathematician, historian, business man, or what not. In fact, attempts to develop him in some such specific direction, and to give him practice in the necessary technique and routine work, may at first entail considerable effort. But as more complete control is acquired over means which lead to artificial ends, as residual traces allow of fuller interpretation, the means come to have a value and a worth because of pleasure and satisfaction which gradually arise out of their control. As the acquired interest grows stronger it replaces the artificial end which at first excited the secondary interest in the means. Many of our scholastic interests have been developed in this manner. The mechanical aspects of much school work is strengthened by artificial ends before the acquired interest is strong enough to hold attention to them. Acquired interest is like primary interest save that it is the result of a secondary interest in the means. Since various objects and situations have by social experience been found to possess value and worth to the individual, and since first contact with such objects or situations may not yield the pleasure and satisfaction which fuller control will bring, it is often necessary to overcome the inertia of the individual by setting artificial ends and incentives and for the time to make the real situations of worth a means to the artificial ends. Fuller control will then be developed and the acquired interest formed.

If possible, acquired interests should be developed from secondary interests of a positive character. If negative interest is used there is danger that the negative aspect may be associated with the means and remain fixed. If these means have social worth, the child should be attracted rather than repelled by them. Thus, a child may do something of a disagreeable nature to avoid the infliction of pain or the performance of still more disagreeable tasks. Some situation, P, is then used to impel secondary interest to disagreeable means, S, which possess their interest simply because they are a means of avoiding P. This is illustrated by the scheme below.

In such a case there is little chance that an acquired interest will be developed in the means.

The whole process, control of means and thought of threatened end, is disagreeable and dissatisfying. The probability is that it will soon be forgotten. One who works unwillingly under threat of punishment will not be impelled to continue such work or to renew old associations with it.

§ IV. EXPLANATION

The motor tendencies, which, as felt, constitute one part of interest, are the expressive side of the sensorimotor unit. The direction in which they point is dependent upon the results of previous experience. Tendencies of appetition towards some situations and of aversion from other situations are due to the feelings of pleasure-pain, satisfaction, dissatisfaction, etc., which resulted from previous control. The appetition or aversion does not make the situation attractive or repelling. The attractive or repelling nature of a situation is due to former experience which has developed meaning in one or the other direction. Representation of the situation will then excite the motor tendencies towards or from it. The strength of such tendencies and the persistence with which they continue may be taken in part as a measure of the impelling or repelling character of the situation.

From a biological point of view, selection and development of some forms of control would be practically impossible without such motor tendencies and attitudes. The gliding about of abstract ideas or cold, formal images can not give rise to the warmth and moving power of interest. Summation of a number can hardly produce what one does not possess as such. All impressions do not and can not have equal impelling power, and if direction and purposive meaning are to be given to some in preference to others, use and function as determined by motor control must be present. If an individual reacted equally to all impressions or ideas of sufficient vividness to force their way into consciousness, he would develop an incoherency of action which would injure or destroy him. Even the most scatter-brained person must cling to some simple interest, must have some tendencies which direct his efforts in a more or less specific direction when situations of a furthering or hindering nature arise. Such interests may be primitive and immediate but they are necessary if the individual is not to be submerged in chaos and confusion. In fact, the vividness and inherent, impelling nature of situations which can result only in harm must be stamped with a proper value, must develop a negative interest, must excite motor tendencies to destroy, or remove, or withdraw from the situation. The clang of the bell on the street, for example, means one thing, that of the bell at home means another, according as the motor attitude points one way or the other.

This purposive character shows the inadequacy of those views which consider interest simply as pleasure-pain. Many situations of inherent, pleasure-pain exciting power may, upon first impression, hold attention for a while, but in short time, wane and die away; and upon further representation, they may fail to excite even a faint glimmer of interest. If reaction towards such situations shows their useless or perhaps harmful nature, their passive and superficial pleasure-pain aspects are passed by or ignored. They will then lack interest in spite of their inherent, impelling nature. This dynamic difference beween pleasure-pain and interest accounts also for the intense interest which may be excited by objects of an apparently commonplace or even repelling character. Objects may lack the surface qualities which attract and first contact with them may yield but little pleasure, may, in fact, be repelling or painful. Were interest simply a feeling of pleasure-pain, etc., such objects would not be able, as they are, to excite a positive interest. It is the use to which such objects can be put, the service which they are able to yield, the pleasure or satisfaction to which they lead, which determines the interest in them. When present, they excite motor tendencies to react in the manner which on previous occasions resulted in pleasure or satisfaction. Since the interest may be present as soon as the object is cognised, and since no pleasure can result until motor control has been realised, the two, pleasure and interest, can hardly be the same. Interest is developed on the bases of pleasure, etc., and instinct, but it is neither of these. A common example is interest in a book, or a golf-stick, or a packing case, or a time-table, etc., which, previous to fuller control, are more or less indifferent as far as pleasure-pain is concerned. Reaction at first may, in fact, have been of a purely instinctive character.[6]

[6] Much of the discussion of the motor and physiological aspects of attention apply to interest. Discussion of these would simply be unnecessary duplication. See Chapter III, 2, and Chapter IV.

CHAPTER VII

THE IDEAL ASPECT OF INTEREST

§ I. DESCRIPTION

In its simplest form, interest on the cognitive side consists of a fringe of meaning or perhaps a dim awareness of the future moment which is to be realised. There need be no distinct image or thought of such a future state. The impressions carry with them, as it were, a wavy, blurred outline of what is to come, a kind of iridescent halo of possibility. When the interest exists, the object is looked at in another light. It means more to the individual. It lingers longer in the center of the attentive field. More often, however, the interesting object or situation excites an image or a train of ideas which point to the future moment which is to be realised. These images or ideas are present at times only as fragments, only as piecemeal signs to point the way. Sometimes they rise, give motor direction, and flit away, leaving only the motor attitude. Often only the verbal image is present. A man who is gazing intently at a railroad time-table may show interest in what, under other circumstances, might not hold the attention for more than a moment. On the cognitive side the interest consists in the images and ideas which are aroused by the directions, figures, etc., in the thoughts of future moments of control which will yield satisfaction or pleasure. The printed schedule may excite anticipations of country life, pleasant rambles, agreeable companions, and the like. It may revive thoughts of work to be accomplished, of engagements to be met, of effort to be put forth, of control which will end in ease, satisfaction or pleasure. The time-table is of interest in that it is able to make connections with future moments which affect the individual. On the ideal side such interest consists of the images and ideas which point to the future situations which are to be realised.

In interest in present, concrete situations, the ideal aspect is merged in the sensory. There is present an ideal trend which is transmitted outwards through motor channels. Thus, as far as the sensory elements are concerned, there is little difference between a trunk or case on the street, and the particular trunk or case in one's room which contains art treasures, books, implements, clothes, hats, or what not. The great difference between them, the difference which constitutes

14

the interest in the one, is the meaning which this one has, the significance which it bears, the anticipation which it excites. This meaning, this pointing outwards to the future, this prospective reference, is often overlooked, because it is so closely connected with the predominating motor attitude. By comparing situations which have interest, with similar situations which have little interest, one can more easily distinguish the ideal aspect of the interest.

Where a situation is more or less ideal, as a thought, a plan, a mental picture, the revived elements are more distinct. They usually exist as free images and ideas. A name, for example, may stir up a host of associations which circulate about the basic thought or image and hold it in the center of attention. The parent who is planning the future of his child, the inventor who is mapping out an outline of some invention, the soldier who is thinking of ways and means to trap the enemy, the student who is working out some problem,—all are examples in point. The ideas or images do not usually arise as clean-cut totalities, with perfect forms and well rounded outlines. Only the faintest glimmer at times is present, sometimes only frayed edges and quickly vanishing traces. When these are insufficient to direct the motor attitude they are made more definite by means of words, drawings, graphic outlines, and the like. Thus, one may repeat and rerepeat a word which is not understood, or may seek further light by drawing out the parts of a problem, and so on. So long as they are vivid enough to direct action, however, they pass along in an even flow without articulatory, manual, or other halts.

Curiosity, expectation and desire. In curiosity, the imagination supplies what the unknown elements in an object or situation are unable to present in themselves. The individual fits now this, now that image or idea to the situation which has attracted him. Since the relation of the object to the future welfare of the individual is partially unknown, he seeks to fill the gap by drawing upon the ideal resources which have been developed from former experiences. The great terror which strikes some when in the presence of a situation almost totally unknown is due in part to their inability to connect it with their personal history. Sometimes a future situation is dimly thought or imagined and the individual then may be in a quiver of excitement to see what are the possibilities of realisation. The curiosity of passers-by is often of such a sort.

When expectation is present, the cognitive aspect of interest consists chiefly in thoughts and ideas of the situation which is to be realised. There are usually numerous imaginative additions which may or may not be realised. These embellishments and added imaginative features give greater impelling power to the situation which is anticipated. The individual who expects presents, honors, promotion, and the like, may magnify them and ideally enhance the possibilities of pleasure and satisfaction to be obtained from them. When no exaggeration is present, the interest centers round some representative idea with the associations which inhere in it. The individual then looks forward to some situation which has arisen before, and calls to mind the pleasing and satisfying incidents connected with it.

In desire, the tendencies excited by the possibilities of realising a future situation may impel the construction of a series of ideal means. Such means serve to connect the future with the present. An individual will then work out a series of carefully coördinated means which will guide him to the situation in view. He may have an interest in the solution of a problem. His desire to solve it may impel him to think of further information to be obtained, of books or persons that will assist him, and so on. Worry, sleeplessness, etc., are often caused by a tumultuous and irresistible flow of ideas which fail to satisfy conditions, bridge the gap between the aim and the present situation, or form a harmonious and consistent system. Interest in the means is present because of their connection with the pleasing or satisfying terminus. On the cognitive side there will be the images, ideas, outlines, etc., of the means, and numerous other associated ideas, as, of the pleasing terminus, of the results of realisation, of similar means or ends, and so on. The mere idea of all that is possible in a future situation will induce interest in associated ideas, will transfer a portion of the interest to other objects or ideas which may aid in the realisation of the situation which is desired.[1]

§ II. ILLUSTRATION

1. LITERARY.

Oh, Day, if I squander a wavelet of thee,
A mite of my twelve hours' treasure,
The least of thy gazes or glances,
(Be they grants thou art bound to or gifts beyond
    measure)
One of thy choices or one of thy chances,

[1] See the discussion in the foregoing chapter.

(Be they tasks God imposed thee or freaks at thy
   pleasure)
—My Day, if I squander such labor or leisure,
Then shame fall on Asolo, mischief on me.

Thy long blue solemn hours serenely flowing,
Whence earth, we feel, gets steady help and good—
Thy fitful sunshine-minutes, coming, going,
As if earth turned from work in gamesome mood—
All shall be mine! But thou must treat me not
As prosperous ones are treated, those who live
At hand here, and enjoy the higher lot,
In readiness to take what thou wilt give,
And free to let alone what thou refusest;
For, Day, my holiday, if thou ill-usest
Me, who am only Pippa,—old year's sorrow,
Cast off last night, will come again to-morrow:
Whereas, if thou prove gentle, I shall borrow
Sufficient strength of thee for new-year's sorrow.

'Pippa Passes.'   Browning.

At half-past seven a little door opened, and a Salvation
Army soldier stuck out his head. "Ayn't no sense
blockin' the wy up that wy," he said. "Those as 'as
tickets cawn come hin now, an' those as 'asn't cawn't
come hin till nine."

Oh, that breakfast! Nine o'clock! An hour and a
half longer! The men who held tickets were greatly
envied. They were permitted to go inside, have a wash,
and sit down and rest until breakfast, while we waited
for the same breakfast on the street.—*The People of the
Abyss*, Jack London, 123.

I well remember the first over-land mail. It was brought by Kit Carson in saddle-bags from Taos in New Mexico. We heard of his arrival at Los Angeles, and waited patiently for his arrival at headquarters. His fame then was at its height, from the publication of Fremont's books, and I was very anxious to see a man who had achieved such feats of daring among the wild animals of the Rocky Mountains, and still wilder Indians of the Plains. At last his arrival was reported at the tavern of Monterey, and I hurried to hunt him up. I cannot express my surprise at beholding a small, stoop-shouldered man, with reddish hair, freckled face, soft blue eyes, and nothing to indicate courage or daring. He spoke but little, and answered questions in monosyllables.—*Memoirs of Gen. W. T. Sherman,* I:74-75.

You know what a university is, and a university degree? It is the necessary hall-mark of a man who wants to do anything in teaching. My scheme, or dream, is to be a university graduate, and then to be ordained. By going to live at Christminster, or near it, I shall be at headquarters, so to speak, and if my scheme is practicable at all, I consider that being on the spot will afford me a better chance of carrying it out than I should have elsewhere.—*Jude the Obscure,* Thomas Hardy, 4.

2. EXPERIMENTAL.

At an election of officers or public officials, note expressions which denote an interest in the outcome. Observe the trend of the discussions, the associations which are aroused, the ideas which are uttered, etc.

In looking through the pages of a 'Reader's Handbook,' or a reference book of 'Phrase and Fable' do you stop at parts and read on? Why do you stop at some names, references, etc., and not at others? What are the associations which determine the halting places, centers of interest, etc.?

When you are interested in some situation, as, a vacation trip, a story, a piece of work, etc., note the associations which are revived, the time to which they refer, their connection with the situation in the focus of attention, and the like.

Why do you work the number of hours which you do? Is it the work itself which impels you to further effort? How is such work connected with the future? What is the aim of the work? What aspects make this aim agreeable and satisfying? What associations revolve about the aim?

Note the different interests which stimulate your efforts. Compare one with the other. Note the associations clustered about each. What are the means to which you attend and which hold your interest because they point to a possibility of realising one or the other ends in view? How have these means been amplified? Have you reflected on them, used words, diagrams, etc., to give you a better view of the situation towards which you are working?

§ III. DEVELOPMENT

The development of the cognitive elements in interest is from impression to image, and from image to organised thought. The residual traces which are left by pleasing or satisfying situations form a basis for imaginative and other, more orderly, cognitive control. Visual, auditory, tactile, and similar residua are left both by the impressions which come from the object or situation and by the manipulation and control which are attempted. According as experience has been more or less extensive, traces may be deposited giving a basis for a series of connected images or a train of thought.

Primary, secondary and acquired interest. In the more elementary stages of development, simple objects or situations which have already excited feelings of pleasure, satisfaction, etc., will, upon representation, arouse ideas and images of the terminal moment towards which control of them will lead. Continued experience with similar situations will form the basis of numerous associations. The mere idea or name may then excite interest in so far as the idea or name is linked with associations which are connected with a pleasurable terminus. An object, which, when controlled, manipulated, etc., yields pleasure or satisfaction, will leave traces which will constitute the basis of further meaning. When the object is again seen, it will excite such traces and become clothed with an interest by virtue of the residua which have been stamped in and intensified by the feelings which the previous control has excited. Since the object and its control yielded pleasure and satisfaction on one occasion, the probability is that it will do likewise upon another. Hence it has fuller meaning and is looked upon with interest. As experience with such an object widens, the object may succeed in rousing images and ideas of pleasing and satisfying moments to which it is able to lead. A child's interest in a toy, a mechanic's interest in a tool, an adult's interest in a scene connected with his childhood days,—all are of this character. In the negative the same holds true. If a situation or object has yielded dissatisfaction or pain, it, too, will revive a meaning, or images or ideas which repel instead of attract. That the burnt child dreads fire is well known.

Should there be a gap between the present situation and a desired terminus, both terminus and present are studied, worked over, reconstructed, and tried in various ways so that the ideal means to bridge the gap may be evolved. The end to be attained, the object desired, the situation to be controlled, or what not, may be removed either in place, in time, or in both. Thus an individual may desire to get at the contents of a trunk, or case, or may try to recover an object which has been thrown over a fence or across a stream. The present situation under immediate control will be tested and examined, means will be sought to bridge the gap between the present and the future moment to be realised, connections will be worked out, and so on. The individual, for example, may seek information of others, may think of implements, may try to recollect similar occasions, may search the vicinity for material, and so on. Interest centers in the means because of their connection with the end in view.

The end may be a potential one and may exist in the more or less distant future. At least there is a strong belief in the possibility of its existence and realisation. Such an end may be ideally constructed out of present experience, from contact with others, reading, observation, and the like. The individual may then desire realisation of his aim, and may set about constructing means and molding the present for the purpose. He may desire a position of responsibility, promotion, material goods, or what not. He may plan further study and work, may consider the advisability of joining societies and

organisations, etc. We may have a whole chain
of connected aims, one leading to the other, and
each realised by a series of means. Thus, *A*
may lead to *B, B* to *C, C* to *D,* and so on. A
student, for example, may be interested in history. If history means for such a person possible intellectual occupation, passing of pleasant
hours, etc., the interest is primary, or perhaps
acquired. But his interest in history may be
secondary. He may see in history the possibility
of passing an examination. Passing of the examination may mean possession of a certificate
or degree. Possession of a certificate or degree
may mean eligibility for another examination,
and so on, to some ultimate realisation, as, ap-
pointment to a position, winning of honors, etc.
This state of affairs can be paralleled in business,
in the home, and elsewhere. Interest in means
which aid in realising any of the ends in view is
then secondary. Many of our interests are of
this nature.

In the course of the various processes leading
to the ultimate realisation, none of the means
may have had any interest or pleasure, *per se.*
In fact, some of them may have been repelling.
During the process of attention to these means,
however, sufficient facts, etc., may remain to

form the basis for the appreciation of new matter. One who studies history from altogether ulterior motives may thus come to find an interest in it as such. So, too, habits of attention to the means may persist and interest in them remain. One who is accustomed to doing work for a considerable length of time will finally come to feel unrest and disturbance if such work is not forthcoming. To regain ease and quiescence, the work will again be desired, and an effort will be put forth to obtain fuller control. Interest of such a sort is acquired. It differs from primary interest only in the fact that it is the result of secondary interest, the residua of the latter.

§ IV. EXPLANATION

The rise of interest is dependent upon the instincts and feelings of the individual, and upon the copies and selection of the social group in which the individual moves. The former aspect has been treated in the preceding chapter. The importance of social guidance and selection remains to be considered. The models which are before an individual give form and direction to his instinctive behavior, and social approval aids in stamping in some reaction to the exclusion of others. The difference between the interests of the slum child and those of his more refined brother are due to a great extent to the difference in the environments which surround them. There is no reason why the slum child should mangle his pronunciation, slip in a patois and slang, and develop interests which are not sanctioned by society at large, other than the stifling environment which surrounds him, and the indifference of the school, which looks upon his acquirements as good enough for him, and which often passes him through its walls, illiterate, unrefined, slovenly, and ignorant, but good at heart and anxious to absorb the best, if only he is given the opportunity to come within its influence. Let 'crap shooting' and profanity be the 'style' in a neighborhood, and innocent children will follow copy without intending harm or knowing the significance of their actions as judged by more cultured individuals. Let the school accept slovenly expression, and careless, dirty work, and it gives its approval to results which even the child himself would not hand in, if trained for a time by proper guidance and selection. In a statistical study of the influences which determined the pursuits of English men of science, Galton found the following:

Number   Due to

59   Innate tastes (*mem:* not necessarily *hereditary*).

11   Fortunate accidents. It will be noticed that these generally testify to the existence of an innate taste.

19   Indirect opportunities and indirect motives.

24   Professional influences to exertion.

34   Encouragement at home of scientific inclinations.

20   Influence and encouragement of private friends and acquaintances.

13   Influence and encouragement of teachers.

8   Travel in distant regions.

3   Residual influences, unclassed.[2]

No doubt, for individuals who are exceptionally efficient, or exceptionally depraved, environment can not do as much as in normal cases. Such exceptional cases, however, are comparatively few. For the great mass of normal individuals, and for the extensive level of common, every-day actions and interests, environment plays the most important part.[3]

[2] Galton, Francis, *English Men of Science,* 149.

[3] On the influence of individual and social imitation, see: Baldwin, J. M., *Ment. Dev. in the Child and the Race,* and *Soc. and Eth. Int.* Bagehot, Walter, *Physics and Politics.* Tarde, G., *The Laws of Imitation,* Eng. tr. by Elsie Clews Parsons. Ross, E. A., *Social Psychology.* See also the discussion in the previous chapter, sections III and IV, and in Chapter III.

CHAPTER VIII

RECAPITULATION

§ I. DEFINITION OF INTEREST

Interest may be briefly defined as follows:

Interest is an attitude taken towards a situation, and characterised (1) by motor tendencies and feelings of expectation, anticipation, and strain, (2) by meaning implicit in the situation or by free images and ideas, and (3) by a reference of attitude and ideal content to some future condition of the self.

The kinds of interest are, (1) curiosity, (2) expectation, and (3) conscious desire.

Curiosity
  Situation present and partially known

Expectation
  Situation future and partially unknown

Desire
  Situation future and known
  Definite effort towards realisation
  Ideal construction of means to lead to end

§ II. OUTLINE OF ASPECTS

Motor

Motor attitude felt as innervation, tendency, or strain

Ideal

Simple awareness in which the meaning is merged in the presentation

Single image or idea of a future moment

System of ideas present as a disposition and evolved as a series

§ III. OUTLINE OF STAGES

The stages of interest are (1) primary, (2) secondary, and (3) acquired.

Primary

A present situation leads directly to feelings of pleasure, satisfaction, etc.

Secondary

Interest inheres in means because of their connection with a future situation which is to result in feelings of pleasure, satisfaction, etc.

Acquired

Means which led to a pleasurable situation, and which roused a secondary interest, hold interest on their own account

The direction of interest in all its stages may be positive or negative.

Positive	*Negative*
The future situation is one of pleasure, satisfaction, etc., and is desired	The future situation is one of pain, dissatisfaction, etc., and is avoided

It is to be noted that when the direction of interest is positive, the means under immediate control may be pleasurable or painful. So long as the terminus is pleasing, satisfying, etc., the interest is positive. In negative interest, the terminus is displeasing or dissatisfying, and is avoided. In such a case, the less of two evils may be selected.

§ IV. INTEREST AND ATTENTION

In the more advanced stages of development, interest and attention run together, but at first, attention is somewhat in the lead. Conditions other than interest are able to impel attention. Thus, intensity of impression and feelings of pleasure-pain can excite primary or instinctive attention. Interest is not then in evidence. But if such instinctive attention results in pleasure, ease, satisfaction, and the like, it lays a basis of interest in such a situation. When the situation is again present there will be a felt tendency to go through the process which resulted in the former feelings of pleasure or satisfaction. In more advanced stages, the interest and the attention are concomitant. Interest is then the impelling aspect, and attention the controlling.

INTEREST	ATTENTION
Motor	*Motor*
Felt attitude which tends to realise a future state	Accommodations and adjustments for more perfect control of a situation
Ideal	*Ideal*
Mental construction of the future moment to be realised, existing as fringe of meaning, simple awareness, or as free ideation	Mental reinforcement of incoming impressions, and ideal guidance of motor control
Objective	*Objective*
Value or worth	Clearness and distinctness

§ V. INTEREST AND FEELING

The following characteristics of interest and feeling may be noted:

Interest	Feeling
Reference to the future	Existence in the present
Motor attitude	Passive moment
Feeling of anticipation and strain	Feeling of pleasure-pain, satisfaction, ease, etc.

§ VI. INTEREST AND EFFORT

Interest impels effort. In that an individual is before a situation which will, when properly controlled, lead to a state of pleasure, ease, and the like, effort will be put forth. There need be no immediate pleasure or satisfaction in such control, so long as the final realisation is more or less pleasurable and satisfying. If the terminus is more painful than the present situation, effort will likewise be shown, so long as such effort leads from the repelling situation. In such a case there is no positive gain, and the terminus is one only in a negative sense. Whatever can be associated with an end which is felt to have worth and value will tend to stimulate effort. If the means, in addition to leading to a pleasurable end, possess an interest of their own, greater effort will be put forth. Effort is nothing more than the subjective and felt aspect of motor control in the process of attention.

PART III
EDUCATION

Part III
Education

CHAPTER IX

ATTENTION IN THE CLASSROOM

§ I. THE GIVEN SITUATION

It seems almost self-evident that, to be attentive, the child must have something definite to which it can attend. The situation, moreover, to which the child is supposed to attend, must be controlled in full by the pupil, if attention is to be wholly present. This implies (1) that the child must be able to react to the object or situation in a sensorimotor manner, and (2) that such reaction and control must correspond in some degree to the character and intent of the situation in question. Practical classroom examples will further elucidate these truths.

Arithmetic. In primary work, each child should be busy measuring desk, books, paper, etc., under guidance of the teacher. Colored paper should be folded, cut, measured, and marked by each child. Each child should be asked to measure the rooms at home, to count the windows in the classroom, to find out by his own efforts how many feet or inches high he is, and the like. In number drill, each child should be given a chance to recite individually. The children should be called up in rows, and each one should be rapidly asked the answer of a problem of the type given. Written work on type problems and examples might be required. In spatial measurements, space should be measured, and not verbal descriptions given by the teacher. In counting, actual concrete series should be counted, and not barren, meaningless, verbal symbols. In intermediate and grammar grade instruction, a similar policy should be followed with greater emphasis on the abstract aspects of the problems. Thus, explanation of problems which involve spatial measurements, necessitates construction of rooms, fields, etc., in paper, measurements worked out on such paper, etc. Fractions should be taught by having each pupil break up unitary wholes into equal parts. Drill on such work requires the solution of a number of problems by the pupils. Such problems should be of the type explained. The visual presentation on the blackboard is good, but it neglects the motor phase of attention.

Spelling. In writing, one sees the words as one writes them. Spelling should therefore be taught with emphasis upon the visual and the motor. Write ten or fifteen words on the board, in columns of five or ten. Let the children write them on paper. Then require the pupils to look at the words, look again with emphasis on difficult combinations of letters, close their eyes and try to see the words. Do this once or twice. Have them repeat the spelling of the words out loud, three or four times. Finally, let the words be written two or three times each. If the children are tested, it will be found that very few will fail. Those who miss should be required to write the misspelled words five or ten times each. This method can be applied to the memorising of lists of any kind, of outlines, of tables in arithmetic, etc. It should replace the monotonous concert recitation still in evidence in many classrooms.

Reading. Content. If possible, the meaning of a piece should be acted out by each pupil. The child should be asked to do what the piece sets forth. He should be required to draw out his own interpretation of what the selection describes. He should try to construct the situation according to the directions given. In addition, pictures, diagrams, etc., should be shown by the teacher. Last of all should come the verbal explanation and lecturing still too common in the classroom.

In teaching the meaning and use of words, a similar method should be followed by the teacher. In addition, the teacher should require the pupils to make some attempt to use the words in their daily conversation, in their compositions, etc. They should be urged to read periodicals, papers, etc., for the purpose of finding sentences which have the words in question. They should keep clippings and paste them in blank books. They should so construct sentences that the meaning of the word is made clear from the context. Such masters of style, as Addison, Irving, etc., should be expounded, and an analysis of their method of explaining words by context, should be made by the teacher. Each pupil should be required to find other words which will take the place of the word selected. In reading, the pupil should be required to find other words which will take the place of the one before him in the text.

Reading. Expression. Each pupil should be allowed to read. Teach only five or ten pupils at a time and give the rest busy work of some kind, as writing of spelling words, tables, etc., illustration in color of some story, test or examination. In teaching proper expression to the group under immediate supervision, repeat the word aloud, show the pupil how to shape the lips, place the tongue, and the like. Write the more difficult words and phrases on the board and let each pupil read them. Correct any errors in enunciation or pronunciation. Give words similar to the ones on the board. Show cards on which such words are written, and let each child repeat the word as soon as it is shown. Since reading involves the rapid expression of visual symbols in articulatory terms, the words and sentences should be read off at once without the interpolation of explanations, reasons, or what not. Let each child then read a sentence or so from the reader or the blackboard. Stop any slovenly expression and call upon the child again if he fails to give the proper expression.

Geography. If the surface of the country is explained let each child model a map in clay or *papier mâché.*[1] See

[1] *Papier mâché* is readily made. Take a newspaper, and cut it into small pieces. Let it soak over night in water. Have a child pound it for some time with a stick or stone. Mix a little

that the child makes an actual slope, tableland, mountain, etc. If the pupil makes a mountain like a stone fence, show him that the water will not drain off and form a river, but will collect in a lake or swamp. Connect such models with the proper names. Thus, tell the pupil to make his RIVER BASIN slope more, or his CARPATHIAN MOUNTAINS higher, or his SICILY more triangular and so on.

Let each pupil classify the industries, materials used, etc. Let him collect labels on cases, cans, etc. Have him draw or trace a map and paste on it the different products. Let him indicate with colored lines the lands to which the products go. Have him construct lists and outlines of such products, exports, imports, and the like. Require him to map out railroad lines, steamship routes, etc., and name them, indicating also the cities which are railroad centers, ports, etc. Have him construct lists of the same.

Let the pupils study the location and names of cities, rivers, etc., in the manner above suggested for spelling. Draw an outline map on the blackboard. Mark and name the important cities. Let the pupils visualise the map and the marks which indicate the cities. Let the children copy the outline, etc., on paper. A rough draft will do. Rub out the names on the board, leaving the marks indicating the cities. Call up the pupils, one at a time, and have each child point to the map when the name of the city is called out. Let the pupils in•

flour-paste or mucilage with the pulp. Press this on the board with the thumb. To insure adhesion, coat the board with mucilage or glue.

their seats watch and compare the answer with the maps before them. Do this in the case of rivers, lakes, etc. Test the pupils by having them write the name of the city, etc., when you point to the map, call out the location, etc.

History. Let the children act out some historical incident or event. Assign parts to a group of children, and let the rest write a report on the characters, what they say, the surroundings, etc. Let each pupil make a drawing of the event, with the necessary names, dates, etc. Have the pupils construct outlines which indicate a series of events in logical connection. Place an outline on the blackboard and have each pupil expand it in composition form. Require each pupil to take his book and trace a series of connected events, as, the events leading to establishment of the British Parliament, the territorial expansion of the United States, etc. Let him give the names connected with such events, the men associated with them, the dates, and so on. Assign each pupil to some topic, and let him read up on it and report to the class. Post his report, or a summary of it, on a bulletin board. Let him read it to the class. Mimeograph it and give each pupil a copy of it. Have each pupil draw the necessary maps, with names, dates, etc.

Science. Let each pupil do the experiment and make his own apparatus, if possible. Crude material will do for the simpler experiments. The old-fashioned 'object lesson' is being replaced by laboratory work. Do not require an inference until a number of experiments has been performed, or until an intensive study has

been made of a few experiments. Thus, in the study
of the action of gravity, the different tests, as, weight
of bodies, pendulum, etc., all lead to a similar inference.
This inference should not be asked for till the whole
series of experiments has been made.

Nature study. Let each child plant a seed in a small
flower pot. Let every pupil handle a flower, or a twig,
or the fur of an animal, or what not. Urge every pupil
to bring in specimens, as stones, wood, seeds, etc. Let
each class have a small space in the school garden for its
own use. Let each class have one or two boxes filled
with earth for the same purpose. Take the children on
excursions to the zoo, the park, the green fields, and the
streams in the neighborhood. Use pictures only when
it is impossible to allow the child to handle the objects
in question. Verbal descriptions are almost worthless.
If the class is to study rainfall, let the children look out
of the window. Point out the clouds. Show the direction of the wind by hanging a streamer outside. Wait
for a rainy day if necessary. Reënforce such instruction by requiring the pupils to draw what they have
seen or handled. Let them draw the growing plant in
color. Let them outline the passage of water through
its forms, as, river, vapor, clouds, rain, etc. Each pupil
should be required to do this.

Grammar. Let each pupil work on type sentences,
parts of speech, etc. Have every child construct a number of sentences like the model. Have him fill in blanks.
Let him diagram according to model. Call up the class,
one row at a time, and have each pupil give the kind

of a sentence required, some word used properly, and
the like. Definition should come last of all. At times
it is unnecessary. Use the method of multiple sense
appeal which is suggested in the case of spelling.

The above directions are by no means complete.
They are simply suggestive of numerous other
devices which any teacher can outline. The following points should be kept in mind: (1) Let
each child have some object or situation under
his immediate control. (2) Let each child react
towards such situation in a sensorimotor manner,
i.e., let him visualise it carefully, handle it, de-
scribe it verbally, etc. (3) Facilitate such control by having material ready, lessons carefully
planned, and so on.

§ II. FACILITATION

1. SIMPLICITY. The work in each subject
should be carefully mapped out by the teacher.
A logical outline should be made, including, (1)
a series of connected topics, causally arranged,
(2) references to standard authorities, and (3)
possible correlations with other subjects in the
grade. In addition there should be a daily plan
of the work to be covered during the day. Such
a plan should be brief, and should have (1) definite topics in each subject which is to receive

attention during the day, (2) type sentences, problems, experiments, etc., and (3) mention of the method to be used in each of the subjects, as, development, drill, or what not. The daily plan will ensure some degree of unitary simplicity, and the term plan some degree of sequential simplicity. In addition, the principal of the school should confer with the teachers and unify the work of the school in the different subjects. The emphasis should be about the same in the subjects all along the line. Where one class is receiving instruction in one phase of arithmetic, for example, and another class of the same grade is doing work very much different, the pupils of these classes will hardly be ready to assimilate instruction in the next grade where perhaps another scheme of instruction is pursued and a different emphasis is placed. The daily plan is now recognised as a necessity, and its absence as an indication of laxity, and generally of inefficiency. When the teacher will give helter-skelter instruction with intermissions of vituperation, the pupils will not be in the best condition to attend to the matter before them. Too many points are flashed before them, there is no persistent presentation of a single topic, and often the things which they should not learn are carefully attendea to, *e.g.*, errors, wrong forms, incorrect models, etc. The teacher should carefully cut up the subject matter into small portions, and use every aid possible to make it clear, as, graphic outline, illustration, blackboard summary, etc. He should hold himself down to the topic at hand and should patiently present it in as many ways as possible. For this, careful preparation is necessary.

2. QUALITY OF THE IMPRESSION. Sharp, clear, and clean-cut presentation should be the general rule in teaching. If the blackboard is used, it should be washed with ink, or ink and water, to ensure a good background. The writing should be firm and neat. No children should be allowed to write matter which is to be studied or copied by the others. Important parts should be written in brightly colored chalk, as, orange, yellow, green, or red. Emphasis might also be secured by underlining or boxing in colored chalk. If pencil or pen is to be used, the ink should be free from dirt, the pencils long and properly sharpened. In speaking, the teacher should be careful to enunciate distinctly, and to express himself carefully and accurately. A hurried, careless, slovenly manner of expression tends to make the children careless and inattentive. These direc-

tions may seem trivial and unnecessary, but they often make the difference between efficiency and inefficiency in some subjects. Note how the pupils will look at the board if there is a neatly colored outline map upon it, or a carefully arranged summary. One can hardly blame a pupil for looking out of the window or under the desk if he has before him a grey, dusty board, or a board hurriedly erased and having upon it scraps and fragments of a former presentation which did not come fully beneath the board rubber. The same is true in other aspects of instruction.

8. TIME. Give the pupil time to absorb what is being presented. Allow some time, however small, for each step in the lesson, from the preliminary signal to the end of the lesson. Give the signal, 'Ready,' and see that each pupil is ready. Present one topic, and make reasonably sure that it has been properly assimilated. Pause a moment, and quiz half a dozen pupils, some poor, some medium. Do not hurry along, and do not rest satisfied if one or two pupils can answer. Do not fret and fume if the results of the first presentation are poor, if over half the class misses, if the per cents range from ten to thirty. Give the children time to learn. Present

16

the same topic again, with perhaps slight additions. Take for granted that children learn very slowly, that if too much is forced upon them, they become distracted, or coolly indifferent. Remember that about one half of the new matter presented is forgotten after the first half hour, two thirds in nine hours, three quarters after six days, and four fifths after a month. Time must be taken for development, time for review, and time for drill.

4. PREADJUSTMENT. Give some signal, as, a tap or a word, to indicate that the lesson is to follow. Moreover, see that the signal is obeyed. Do not pass from one lesson to another without having all the pupils prepared to take up the new work. If the one lesson is a writing lesson, and the following is a geography or a history lesson, give some such directions as the following: Pencils down. Pass papers. Books away. Take modeling boards. And so on. Pause slightly after each direction. See that it is followed. If the directions are given in sharp, military fashion, and are followed by a slight pause, they impel attention and set the pupil in a business-like frame of mind. If necessary, make sure that each pupil is in the proper attitude for the new work, by passing rapidly

through one or two of the side aisles. If the
teacher is satisfied to talk ahead with a large
percentage of the children playing under the
desk, writing, finishing up the previous lesson,
and the like, much of his work will be wasted as
far as the attention of the pupils is concerned.
Fixation should be facilitated by having a definite model before the pupils, by calling their
attention to specific aspects of it, by pointing to
the parts which are essential, and so on. A series
of rapid questions will aid in holding the children
in the attitude of attention. Note the external
signs of preadjustment, as, head erect, eyes looking at the object before them, body leaning
slightly forward, etc. Do not continue the
lesson if the majority of the pupils are not in
the right attitude of fixation.

5. IDEAL REINFORCEMENT. Have the blackboard covered with work as soon as the pupils
enter the room. Examples in arithmetic or
grammar, a colored map, colored designs in
drawing, spelling list, etc., should be on the
board before the pupils come. This work should
be connected with the lessons of the day. Home
work, on the other hand, should not be given till
the close of the day. Pupils can not be expected
to attend so closely to the lessons of the day if

they are thinking of problems, etc., to be done at home. Often pupils will be found surreptitiously doing such home work under the desk. In the course of instruction, use the experiences of the child and the objects of the immediate environment in making clear the topics of the lesson. The streams in the gutters, the lake in the park, the stones of the school or other buildings, the clothes worn by the children, the foods which they eat, the labels and marks on manufactured articles, etc., should be used as examples in the presentation of topics in geography, etc. The words in spelling should be selected from the exercises in reading, from the expressions used in arithmetic and grammar, from the lessons in geography and history, from the vocabulary which the children ought to have, etc. Such lists should be revised each term. Composition should be based on work of the term which has been already covered, on experiences of the children, on activities which are within the child's understanding and which are taking place under his eyes, and the like. The teacher should try to find the mental background which will best serve to hold the topic in the focus of attention, which will best enable the presentation to persist. New topics which have little connection with the experiences or the environments of the children will have little chance to continue in the centre of the attentive field.

6. PRACTICE. Practice is necessary to enable ideal backgrounds to persist, and to make habitual the motor coördinations and adjustments which are necessary in attention. The rate of forgetting[2] is so rapid that constant drill is necessary. The rules for drill are as follows: (1) Present *one topic*. Allow for review by giving a few types of the kind already presented, but let the body of the lesson deal with the topic which is to be drilled upon. (2) Secure *repetition*. Let every pupil recite. Call the class up in rows and have each child answer. Give a number of problems or examples of the same kind, and let the children work them. Let the children use blank maps and fill in railroad centres one day, industries another, etc., connecting one with the other. Present similar topics in a series of lessons. Check the problems or types on which most of the children fail, and give them again. Use the method of multiple sense appeal in fastening essential facts in the different subjects. (3) See that such repetition is

[2] See Myers, C. S., *A Text-Book of Experimental Psychology*, Ch. XIII.

properly distributed. If the children do not seem able to grasp the point of the lesson at the end of half an hour, do not continue for an hour or two more. Simplify the work still more, wait for a day or two and try again. Give intermissions so that the children can rest. If two hours are to be spent on some topic, divide the time into half or three-quarter hour periods and spread them over several days. (4) There should be a *mass of material* at hand, and such material should deal with the same topic. The blackboard should be covered with work. Numerous specimens should be on hand. Copies of designs should be ready for distribution. Whatever be the subject, the teacher should see that sufficient material is ready for illustration, use, or what not. No teacher should be satisfied to 'know about what he is going to teach,' or to 'carry the day's work in his head.' (5) Appeal to each pupil through as many of the senses as possible. Let the children visualise, articulate, express themselves manually, listen to the presentation or explanation, etc. Let each sensory impression be followed by some form of motor expression. Let the children do many examples. Let them draw or model many maps. Let them answer in composition form when writing on historical or geographical topics. Let them synopsise and expand stories which have been illustrated, read, and explained. The teacher should plan work to fit the different senses, and such appeals should deal with the same topics.[3]

7. FATIGUE AND PAUSE. So that the children should not be unnecessarily fatigued by the day's work, some consideration should be given to the order in which the subjects are presented. Construction of a proper daily schedule involves (1) the physiological rhythm to which the child is subject, (2) the relative difficulty of the subjects, (3) the length of the period during which instruction is to continue, (4) the distribution of periods over the days of the week, (5) the days of the week most favorable to work, (6) the age and maturity of the children, and (7) general factors, as, the weather, the rhythm of energy during the months of the year, etc.

(a) *Daily rhythm.* The periods of the day most favorable to work are the former half of the morning and the latter half of the afternoon. The morning period again is better than the afternoon period. The best period of the day is from nine to eleven in the forenoon. The

[3] See Arnold, F., *Text-book of School and Class Management,* 1:Ch. V, § III, 3.

second best period is after two in the afternoon.
The end of the morning session and the beginning of the afternoon session are most unfavorable to heavy work.[4]

(b) *Relative difficulty of subjects.* In the
order given, the following subjects put the children to the greatest strain: (1) exercises which
involve muscular effort, as gymnastics, (2) abstract and formal subjects, as arithmetic, grammar, etc., and (3) thought work and exercises
which involve the memory. The kinds of work
which require less energy are, (1) manual work,
as drawing, construction, etc., (2) oral work,
and (3) work which involves content and objective phases rather than formal, as geography,
history, literature, etc. No subject which puts
the child to a special strain should be given at
the end of the morning or the beginning of the
afternoon, and no two such subjects should follow each other.

(c) *Length of periods.* The length of a lesson should vary between fifteen minutes and an
hour or so. Subjects which require less energy
should be given longer periods than subjects
which are more difficult. Forty minutes is con-

---

[4] See O'Shea, M. V., *Dynamic Factors in Education*, 286.
Bagley, W. C., *The Educative Process*, 340.

sidered a normal period for older children, and fifteen or twenty minutes one for younger children. A succession of short periods should be avoided if possible, as this tends to give a choppy effect to the day's work and to produce restlessness.

(d) *Difference in days.* Monday and Friday are not so good as the other days of the week. Less difficult subjects should be given on these days. Days which immediately precede or follow holidays, etc., are also not good for difficult work.

(e) *Maturity of the children.* The age and maturity of the children will condition the length of the periods, the number of intermissions for physical exercise, the length of time for recess, and the general method of instruction which is to be followed. There should be a two-minute setting-up exercise at the end of each lesson. For younger children, there should be a ten or fifteen minute period for play and exercise at about half-past ten, and a similar period after two. Primary periods of instruction should run from fifteen minutes to half or three quarters of an hour. Grammar or intermediate periods should vary between three quarters of an hour and an hour and a half.

(*f*) *Weather influences.* Sultry days and hot days are not favorable to heavy work. The beginning of a snow storm makes the children restless. Days which are cold and clear are favorable to good work. On unfavorable days the teacher should not take up advance work in the difficult subjects. He should review, drill upon, or test old work, give written exercises, etc. Extra effort should be put forth on such days.

(*g*) *Seasonal rhythm.* The best work can be done during the period from December to April. The heaviest work should therefore be done during the last two months of the first term and the first two months of the second term. During the months of June, July, and August, and to a certain extent during the spring months the children show greater excitement and more numerous tendencies to irresponsible action. Crimes, popular outbursts, riots, revolutions, etc., usually break out during the Spring and Summer months.[5]

8. HUNGER AND UNDERFEEDING. Where underfeeding is evident, *i.e.*, where children are underweight, not so much should be expected of

---

[5] See Hall, G. S., *Adolescence*, 2:47. Leffingwell, Albert, *Influence of Seasons upon Conduct.* See also Arnold, F., *Sch. and Cl. Man.*, 2:Ch. I, § IV, 4.

them. If possible underfed or improperly fed children should be given a glass of milk and a biscuit or roll in the morning, at twelve, and at the close of the day. Such food should be given at cost price. From a nutritive point of view soup is not worth much. As Barr points out, 'statistics show that 10 ounces of bread and 1 pint of skimmed milk equal in nutriment a diet composed of 8 ounces of soup, 2 ounces of beef, 2 ounces of potatoes, 1 ounce of turnips, 4 ounces of bread, ½ ounce of butter, and 1 cup of coffee containing 1 ounce of milk and ½ ounce of sugar.'[6]

9. OBSTRUCTED BREATHING. If the child shows signs of obstructed breathing, he should be examined and sent to the school physician. The teacher should also see that the room is properly ventilated

10. WEAK MINDEDNESS. Instruction of weak minded children should use concrete means of presentation in all the subjects. Arithmetic should be taught by means of scissor work, paper folding, colored blocks, etc. Processes should be simple and should, if necessary, be reduced to counting. Counting, in fact, should be used to test the more difficult processes. In language

[6] Barr, M. W., *Mental Defectives*, 170.

work, pictures, illustrations, dramatisations, social activities, modeling in sand, construction work, etc., should be made the basis of oral and written composition, spelling, etc. Only one simple topic in any subject should be presented at a time. Lesson periods should be very short. They may vary between ten minutes and an hour. There should be intermissions in which games are played, social activities conducted, 'make-believe' occupations carried on, and the like. The surroundings of the children should be used as a basis of these different activities.

11. EXTRANEOUS STIMULATION. As soon as the pupil enters the room he should see on the blackboard a general outline of the work of the day. Examples, map, etc., should be on the board. During the lesson the teacher should see that only such material as is necessary for the work is under the pupil's immediate control. The lesson should run on without interruptions. There should be no halts due to missing pencils or pens, empty ink wells, etc. Before the work of the day begins, the teacher or a monitor should arrange such supplies as will be needed during the day. The room should be tidy. Whatever decorations are used, they should be neatly placed. There should be a gen-

eral cleaning-up at least once a week. Loose paper, material, etc. should not lie on the window sills, or desks. The directions given above for preadjustment will be found useful in shutting out sources of extraneous stimulation.[7]

[7] Among others, see the progressive *School Reports* of W. H. Maxwell, New York, J. H. van Sickle, Baltimore, and the *Child Study Reports* of F. W. Smedley, D. P. MacMillan, and F. G. Bruner, Chicago. A similar point of view has been worked out by W. E. Grady, in 'Pragmatic Concepts, and the Educational Process,' New York. The above chapter will probably be further amplified as portion of a volume on general method in instruction.

CHAPTER X

INTEREST IN THE CLASSROOM

§ I. POSITIVE VERSUS NEGATIVE INTEREST

There is nothing very mysterious or uncanny in the development of interest in the classroom. In its simplest terms, the problem is somewhat as follows: Arrange the instruction and discipline in such a manner that whatever the pupil does ends in pleasure, satisfaction, ease, or quiescence. If the activity itself does not so end, then produce pleasure, satisfaction, ease, or quiescence by artificial means. It is a mistaken idea that the child should do his work at school merely because the teacher says so, or that some high and mighty virtue should impel him to do the work. The teacher himself asks for some recompense, and we find very few individuals who will put forth continued effort on the mere say-so of another. The aim of the work in part is the development of obedience to authority, of respect for the true, the good, and the beautiful, etc., but the realisation of this aim calls for laborious effort on the part of the teacher. Many of us, in spite of the efforts of the school, are still painfully lacking in many of the virtues which we too readily take for granted in the child. We must begin from lower levels, and appeal to bases, which, from a more advanced stage, might seem somewhat crass and selfish.

If the work itself does not end in pleasure, satisfaction, etc., and if the teacher does not use artificial means to secure a pleasurable or satisfying result, then the work becomes a drudgery which is done to avoid some greater evil, as, detention, nagging, corporal punishment, and the like. The principal, the parent, the truant officer, and the police court are then called into service to browbeat parent and child, and by threat of fine or imprisonment, to coerce the child to attend to his work at school. Many cases of truancy will always be found, no matter what the school can do either positively or negatively. But the artificial conditions which exist, in which the children consider the school somewhat as a necessary evil, would hardly be found if the school made a systematic attempt to use positive instead of negative interest. There is no inherent virtue in doing a task because the completion of such a task will relieve the child from coercion, punishment, or what not. By association the child will not be led to care for the work. If the task itself is disagreeable, it will have little power of its own to impel the child to continue it, or to attempt it again. No matter how necessary the work may be, if the child does not see the necessity of it, and if the efforts put forth lead to nothing positive in the way of pleasure, ease, satisfaction, etc., the pupil will not feel impelled to strive along similar lines.

Where the children have proper homes, and parents who are interested in their welfare, much of such satisfaction, pleasure, etc., as is needed in the development of interest, is obtained from relatives, and friends who look after the child. But where the children do not have such congenial surroundings, where families of four or five live in two or three rooms, where the boys and girls roam the streets as preferable to close and stuffy rooms, the home can not be depended upon to support the school in the development of interest in school studies. If the school does not use positive means of developing interest, such negative means as beating, detention at court or truant school, etc., are called upon properly to subdue the children.

The use of positive means does not preclude earnest effort, or hard work. The point is not that the work should be made easy, or that everything which is done in the classroom should be pleasurable, but that whatever is done by the children, no matter how difficult or disagreeable, should end in feelings of pleasure or satisfaction. Children will be found the last to shirk hard work which leads to a satisfying or pleasurable terminus. In this sense interest does not conflict with effort, but rather is a means of calling forth the greatest amount of effort.

§ II. APPROVAL AND DISAPPROVAL

1. EXHIBITION OF WORK. When the child has put forth effort on written or similar work, it should be hung up on the walls of the classroom, if only for a short time. The teacher should arrange picture wire, burlap, cardboard, etc., so that arithmetic papers, drawings, construction work, and the like can be exhibited. If the child sees that his efforts are thus appreciated, he will feel satisfied and pleased, and will strive all the more on following occasions. If his work is not quite what it ought to be, refusal to hang it up will have the effect of disapproval. Every means of approval which the teacher uses can thus become a means of disapproval.

2. COMMENDATION. The teacher should not hesitate to praise good work whenever he sees it.

17

He should hold up a good paper before the class and publicly approve the child who has done it. Such expressions as 'Good,' 'Very fine,' 'Excellent,' and the like should be used again and again. A child will feel impelled to work harder if he sees that his efforts receive recognition. On the other hand, continual faultfinding, vituperation, and nagging will discourage him, and finally make him indifferent and callous.

3. MARK. Most of the written work of the pupils, as drawings, compositions, test papers, etc., should be marked by either the teacher or a pupil, and returned to the children. If any papers are thrown away, they should not be destroyed in the presence of the children. Credits might be given for neatness, high per cents, etc. Weekly or monthly ratings in four or five groups of subjects should be posted where all the children can see them. Honor rolls, gold-star charts, etc., are some of the devices by which attention can be called to special merit. If the work is not quite up to the mark, withholding of approval will act as disapproval. Demerits might also be given to check careless work.[1]

[1] For a full discussion of the means of approval and disapproval, see, Arnold, F., *Sch. and Cl. Man.*, 1:Ch. XI.

§ III. SELF-ACTIVITY

Wherever possible the child himself should be allowed to do the work demanded by the lesson. Let the pupil fold paper to illustrate fractions, or arrange splints in groups for counting, or cut out cardboard to illustrate surface measurement of a room, etc. Let him model a map in clay or *papier mâché*, cut it out in colored paper, draw and color it, fill in cities, rivers, etc., paste on samples of products, form lists and outlines, and the like. Let him give sentences in grammar, fill in blanks with the proper forms, diagram, etc. Let him construct apparatus for experiments in science, bring in specimens for nature study, and so on. In addition, cap his efforts with pleasure and satisfaction by publicly praising his work, exhibiting it, marking it, and the like. Do not force him to sit quiet doing nothing, while words, words, words, are being showered upon him. The least thing which will relieve the children from the too common verbiage of the classroom will stimulate and excite them to put forth effort.

§ IV. IMITATION

To guide the self-activity of the children along definite channels, models should be shown them. The best model or copy to stimulate the activity of the children is an actual, concrete situation, of the kind which they are to manipulate. Let them count real money, or paper money. Let them buy and sell as men buy and sell outside of the school, with a pupil as storekeeper, and other children as customers. Let the pupils measure the walls of the classroom, estimate the number of square feet in the surface of the walls, etc. Bring in real leaves and flowers for design work. Let the children handle and test the kinds of stone, wood, fur, cloths, etc., which form the subject matter for geography, nature study, or other lessons. If it is not possible to present concrete situations, use the next-best means of presentation, as, colored illustrations or photographs, diagrams, outlines, and the like. Magazines now reproduce in color many interesting views, and each teacher can readily collect a number of such views. Pupils, too, can be asked to get such pictures. History, geography, literature, reading, etc., will acquire fresh interest by such means.

For review or drill, as in arithmetic or grammar, a problem should be written on the blackboard and its solution indicated below. In addition, the teacher should work out the same problem, step by step, in the presence of the children. They should then be set to work a number of similar problems. The children who work most neatly and correctly should be commended, and their papers should be exhibited. Interest in most of such drill work will be of a secondary nature. No doubt the children have some natural interest in number work as such, but this is rather flitting and unreliable. To ensure the regularity and persistence which are necessary in drill work, secondary interest must be employed. The same holds for other subjects, as, grammar, spelling, and the like.

§ V. MULTIPLE SENSE APPEAL

In the presentation of a new lesson and in drill on an old one, appeals should be made to as many of the senses as possible. The pupil should see pictures, maps, outlines, models, etc. He should be allowed to visualise them for a definite period. Essential aspects should be pointed out to him, and he should be urged to look, close his eyes, revive the impression, and look again to see how correctly he has reproduced the visual presentation. He should then model, draw, write, etc. Oral expression might be required. After the sensory appeals have been made, the pupils might be required to express themselves in composition form either orally or in writing. Commendation, exhibition of work, etc., will increase whatever satsfaction or pleasure the work itself has produced.

§ VI. INTEREST AND THE CURRICULUM

Experimental tests and empirical observation in the classroom will show that pupils differ in natural ability and talent. Some will be found strong in one group of subjects, others in another group of subjects. Pupils will differ in their ability in the same subject. A pupil who is good in division, is not necessarily good in addition or multiplication. One good in grammar or composition may be found weak in spelling or reading. We should not strive, therefore, to do the impossible, to level all differences, and to create an equal interest in all the subjects in all pupils. The most we can do is to ask for minimum requirements in such subjects as are required by society at large, and to allow the pupils to develop their natural talents along special lines. By approval, guidance of self-activity, presentation of the proper models, etc., we can stimulate pupils to exert effort in all the subjects to a minimum degree, and in special subjects to a maximum degree. The minimum should be the same for all pupils, but the maximum will differ according to the ability and inclination of the special pupil concerned. Classification and promotion should not be based on an average, but on minimum proficiency in most of the subjects, and greater proficiency in one or two in which the pupil shows greatest interest.

The problem of the teacher is to develop natural tendencies into definite interests. The bases to which he must appeal are the instincts and feelings of the child. Appeal to the child's interest is possible only after some interest has been already developed. The child does not come with interests ready-made to which appeal can be made. Rather, he comes with blind and inchoate tendencies, wild strivings, formless instincts, which the teacher must direct and shape. By presentation of models, by guidance of the child's self-activity, by capping his efforts with satisfaction, the teacher fashions the instincts of the pupil, shows him that his efforts are worth while, and develops interests which can be of service in the direction of further effort.[1]

[1] Compare DeGarmo, C., *Interest and Education.*

INDEX OF NAMES

INDEX OF SUBJECTS

A LIST OF BOOKS FOR TEACHERS

ARNOLD, FELIX. **A Text Book of School and Class Management.**
Theory and Practice. *Cloth. 12mo. xxii+409 pages. Index. $1.25 net.*

BAGLEY, WILLIAM CHANDLER. **Classroom Management: Its Principles
and Technique.** By William Chandler Bagley, Superintendent of the
Training Department, State Normal School, Oswego, N. Y.
Cloth. 12mo. xviii+352 pages. $1.25 net.

——**The Educative Process.** *Cloth. 12mo. xix+358 pages. $1.25 net.*

BROWN, JOHN FRANKLIN. **The American High School.** By John Frank-
lin Brown, Ph.D., formerly Professor in Education and Inspector of High
Schools for the State University of Iowa.
Cloth. xii+498 pages. 12mo. $1.25 net.

CHUBB, PERCIVAL. **The Teaching of English.** By Percival Chubb, Principal of High School Department, Ethical Culture School, New York.
Cloth. 12mo. xvii+411 pages. $1.00 net.

COLLAR, GEORGE, AND CROOK, CHARLES W. **School Management and
Methods of Instruction.** By George Collar and Charles W. Crook,
London. *Cloth. 12mo. viii+336 pages. $1.00 net.*

CRONSON, BERNARD. **Methods in Elementary School Studies.** By
Bernard Cronson, A.B., Ph.D., Principal of Public School No. 3, Borough
of Manhattan, City of New York. *Cloth. 12mo. 167 pages. $1.25 net.*

——**Pupil Self-Government.** *Cloth. 12mo. ix+107 pages. $.90 net.*

CUBBERLEY. **Syllabus of Lectures on the History of Education.** With
Selected Bibliographies and Suggested Readings. By Ellwood P. Cub-
berley. Second Edition, revised and enlarged. In two parts.
Part I, v+129 pages, $1.50 net; Part II, xv+361 pages, $1.50 net.
Complete in one volume, $2.60 net.

DE GARMO, CHARLES. **Interest and Education.** By Charles De Garmo,
Professor of the Science and Art of Education in Cornell University.
Cloth. 12mo. xvii+230 pages. $1.00 net.

——**The Principles of Secondary Education.**
Vol. I, Studies. Cloth. 12mo. xii+299 pages. $1.25 net.
Vol. II, Processes of Instruction. xii+200 pages. $1.00 net.
Vol. III, Processes of Instruction. In press

DUTTON, SAMUEL T. **Social Phases of Education in the School and the
Home.** By Samuel T. Dutton, Superintendent of the Horace Mann
Schools, New York. *Cloth. 12mo. ix+259 pages. $1.25 net.*

DUTTON & SNEDDEN. **The Administration of Public Education in the
United States.** By Samuel Train Dutton, A.M., and David Snedden,
Ph.D. With an Introduction by Nicholas Murray Butler, Ph.D., LL.D.
Cloth. viii+595 pages. Bibliography. Index. 12mo. $1.75 net.

FITCH, SIR JOSHUA. **Educational Aims and Methods.** Lectures and Ad-
dresses by Sir Joshua Fitch, late Her Majesty's Inspector of Training
Colleges. *Cloth. xii+448 pages. 12mo. $1.25 net.*

——**Lectures on Teaching.** *Cloth. xiii+393 pages. 16mo. $1.00 net.*

GRAVES, FRANK P. **A History of Education before the Middle Ages.** By
Frank Pierrepont Graves, Ohio State University.
Cloth. 320 pages. Bibliography. $1.10 net.

HALLECK, REUBEN POST. **The Education of the Central Nervous System.**
A Study of Foundations, especially of Sensory and Motor Training. By
Reuben Post Halleck, M.A. (Yale).
Cloth. 12mo. xii+258 pages. $1.00 net.

A LIST OF BOOKS FOR TEACHERS—*Continued*

HANUS, PAUL H. **A Modern School.** By Paul H. Hanus, Professor of the History and Art of Teaching in Harvard University.
Cloth. 12mo x+306 pages. $1.25 net.

——**Educational Aims and Educational Values.** By Paul H. Hanus.
Cloth. 12mo. vii+221 pages. $1.00 net.

HERBART, JOHN FREDERICK. **Outlines of Educational Doctrine.** By John Frederick Herbart. Translated by Alex. F. Lange, Associate Professor of English and Scandinavian Philology and Dean of the Faculty of the College of Letters, University of California. Annotated by Charles De-Garmo, Professor of the Science and Art of Education, Cornell University.
Cloth. Large 12mo. xi+334 pages. $1.25 net.

HORNE, HERMAN HARRELL. **The Philosophy of Education.** By Herman Harrell Horne, Assistant Professor of Philosophy and Pedagogy in Dartmouth College.
Cloth. 8vo. xvii+295 pages. $1.50 net

——**The Psychological Principles of Education.** By Herman Harrell Horne.
Cloth. 12mo. xiii+435 pages. $1.75 net.

HUEY, EDMUND B. **The Psychology and Pedagogy of Reading.** By Professor Edmund B. Huey, of the Western University of Pennsylvania.
Cloth, 12mo. xvi+469 pages. $1.40 net

JONES. OLIVE M., LEARY, ELEANOR G., and QUISK, AGNES E. **Teaching Children to Study.** The Group System applied.
Illustrated. Cloth. viii+193 pages. 12mo. $.80 net.

KILPATRICK, VAN EVRIE. **Departmental Teaching in Elementary Schools.** By Van Evrie Kilpatrick.
Cloth. 12mo. xiii+130 pages. 16mo. $.60 net.

KIRKPATRICK, EDWIN A. **Fundamentals of Child Study.** By Professor Edwin A. Kirkpatrick, Principal of State Normal School, Fitchburg, Mass.
Cloth. 12mo. xxi+384 pages. $1.25 net.

MAJOR, DAVID R. **First Steps in Mental Growth.** A Series of Studies in the Psychology of Infancy. By David R. Major, Professor of Education in the Ohio State University.
Cloth xiv+360 pages. 12mo. $1.25 net.

THE McMURRY SERIES
Each, cloth, 12mo.

General Method.

——**The Elements of General Method.** By Charles A. McMurry.
323 pages. $.90 net.

——**The Method of the Recitation.** By Charles A. McMurry and Frank M. McMurry, Professor of the Theory and Practice of Teaching, Teachers College, Columbia University.
xi+329 pages. $.90 net.

Special Method. By Charles A. McMurry.

—— **Special Method in Primary Reading and Oral Work with Stories.**
vii+103 pages. $.60 net

——**Special Method in the Reading of English Classics.**
vi+254 pages. $.75 net.

—— **Special Method in Languages in the Eight Grades.**
viii+192 pages. $.70 net.

—— **Course of Study in the Eight Grades.**
Vol. I.   Grades I to IV. vii+236 pages. $.75 net.
Vol. II. Grades V to VIII. v+226 pages. $.75 net.

—— **Special Method in History.**
vii+291 pages. $.75 net.

—— **Special Method in Arithmetic.**
vii+225 pages. $.70 net.

—— **Special Method in Geography.**
xi+217 pages. $.70 net.

—— **Special Method in Elementary Science.**
ix+75 pages. $.75 net.

—— **Nature Study Lessons for Primary Grades.** By Mrs. Lida B. McMurry, with an introduction by Charles A. McMurry.
xi+191 pages. $.60 net.

A LIST OF BOOKS FOR TEACHERS—*Continued*

MONROE, PAUL. **A Brief Course in the History of Education.** By Paul Monroe, Ph.D., Professor in the History of Education, Teachers College, Columbia University. *Cloth. 8vo. xviii+409 pages. $1.25 net.*

—— **A Text-Book in the History of Education.**
Cloth. xxiii+277 pages. 12mo. $1.90 net.

—— **A Source Book of the History of Education.** For the Greek and Roman Period. *Cloth. xiii+515 pages. 8vo. $1.25 net.*

O'SHEA, M. V. **Dynamic Factors in Education.** By M. V. O'Shea, Professor of the Science and Art of Education, University of Wisconsin.
Cloth. 12mo. xiii+320 pages. $1.25 net.

—— **Linguistic Development and Education.**
Cloth. 12mo. xvii+347 pages. $1.25 net.

PARK, JOSEPH C. **Educational Woodworking for Home and School.** By Joseph C. Park, State Normal and Training School, Oswego, N. Y.
Cloth. 12mo. xiii+310 pages, illus. $1.00 net.

PERRY, ARTHUR C. **The Management of a City School.** By Arthur C. Perry, Jr., Ph.D., Principal of Public School No. 85, Brooklyn, N. Y.
Cloth. 12mo. viii+350 pages. $1.25 net.

ROWE, STUART H. **The Physical Nature of the Child.** By Dr. Stuart H. Rowe, Professor of Psychology and the History of Education, Training School for Teachers, Brooklyn, N. Y.
Cloth. 12mo. vi+211 pages. $.90 net

SMITH, DAVID E. **The Teaching of Elementary Mathematics.** By David E. Smith, Professor of Mathematics, Teachers College, Columbia University. *Cloth. xv+312 pages. 12mo. $1.00 net.*

SNEDDEN AND ALLEN. **School Reports and School Efficiency.** By David S. Snedden, Ph.D., and William H. Allen, Ph.D. For the New York Committee on Physical Welfare of School Children.
Cloth. 12mo. xi+183 pages. $1.50 net.

VANDEWALKER, NINA C. **The Kindergarten in American Education.** By Nina C. Vandewalker, Director of Kindergarten Training Department. Milwaukee State Normal School.
Cloth. xiii+274 pages. Portr., index, 12 mo. $1.25 net.

WARNER, FRANCIS. **The Study of Children and Their School Training.** By Francis Warner. *Cloth. xix+264 pages. 12mo. $1.00 net.*

WINTERBURN AND BARR. **Methods in Teaching.** Being the Stockton Methods in Elementary Schools. By Mrs. Rosa V. Winterburn, of Los Angeles, and James A. Barr, Superintendent of Schools at Stockton, Cal.
Cloth. xii+355 pages. 12mo. $1.25 net.

Published By

THE MACMILLAN COMPANY

64-66 Fifth Avenue, New York